SAFE

at

First

PAMELA M.

ISBN 979-8-88540-842-4 (paperback)
ISBN 979-8-88540-843-1 (digital)

Christian Faith Publishing
832 Park Avenue
Meadville, PA 16335
www.christianfaithpublishing.com

Printed in the United States of America

PREFACE

This book was inspired not only by the Holy Spirit but also by the interactions and encouragement of those experiencing cancer, directly or indirectly. They expressed their opinions that what I had to say was worth sharing. In no way is this book meant to point fingers, criticize, condemn, or degrade anyone or any measure of response.

We all have to fight our own battles in our own way. It is simply a way of presenting a different point of view and expressing gratitude to all that were vital during my ordeal. If just one person or family is uplifted by reading this book, then the efforts to produce it will be worthwhile. God bless all who experience this indiscriminate disease in any way.

INTRODUCTION

Writing this book was inspired, but there came a time when, presented with the contract, I questioned if I was following God's plan. I always had difficulty asking for help even from my son, who had been very generous over the years. This time, I knew he wasn't the answer, so I tested God's involvement. I made a deal with myself (and God, maybe). I decided to drive by the credit union and see if my friend Janice was in her office, which could be seen from the street. If she was there, like she had been so many other times, I would meet with her to secure a personal loan; but if she wasn't, I would drive home and forget the whole thing. You guessed it—she was there, stepping in again as one of God's angels. His timing is always perfect even when we don't think so. I had worked to improve my credit, and my loans were almost paid off. This was the right time—His time.

CHAPTER 1

First Base

Sunday morning and the field was prime for play. The sun was warming the air, teased by the trade winds that prompted rival temperatures. Small spirals of dust glanced across the bases as the grass glistened with fresh acceptance of a new day. Players assumed their positions as the pitcher ascended the mound. A few practice pitches, then the umpire's call rang out, "Batter up!"

Watching the first batter take command of the batter's box, like a bird confident in its nest, my stomach fluttered with nervous expectancy. "Strike one" rang through the air as the batter swung and missed. No call for the next pitch that exceeded the strike zone, and the batter prepared once more. *Crack!* The sound of the bat meeting the ball, which sailed out over the shortstop. The center fielder raced for the ball but got control of it only after the runner was safe on second. Every player in the dugout cheered as the next batter stepped up to the plate. A high fly ball proved a sacrifice fly, as the runner tagged up and raced for third. A few more batters resulted in one run and an additional out. Without hesitation, I was called to the batter's box.

The day was warm and breezy, lending outside forces to the already stressful situation. My anxiety level went through the roof. Hands sweaty, mouth dry, and a grip on the bat I hadn't felt in years settled in. I set my feet back from the edge of the plate and swung the bat slowly to get its feel. The pitcher smiled and let go of the ball as my heart raced. My reaction time was off, and I swung ahead of the ball. The guys had given me a light bat, and this was slow pitch. Having played fast pitch for years, my habits would prove resistant. I stepped out of the batter's box for a moment to gather my courage. Wanting to run and give up this foolish venture, I took a deep breath remembering my high school days of twenty years past and watched carefully as the second ball flew by, catching me by surprise, and the call graced the air, "Strike."

The next ball resembled a memory of the past—high and outside, my specialty. One of the most exhilarating feelings is that minute point when the sphere meets the cylinder and sends the ball hurtling. As I stretched out with the bat, the connection sounded and the ball left the area ascending into the center field, over the head of the second basemen. Astounded, I froze for a moment and then took off toward first base. Slinging the bat to the ground as I ran, it seemed as though the base stretched out before me in an unreachable state. My legs were weak but taken over by a vengeance for success. To my amazement, a few more strides and as my cleat graced the base, I heard that wonderful cry, "Safe." Running through then returning, I stood panting but felt elated. Standing on the base, I waited with a feeling of great exhilaration as I heard the cheering from my dugout. As I felt the support of my team, I thought to myself, *If they only knew.* They did not suspect that this was a great day of superb success. This proved to be a personal best.

Feelings of joy and surprise filled my mind as the thoughts of the past came pouring in. Just months ago, this feat would have been impossible. Flashes of the past came over me as I relived the days when walking ten feet brought about gasping for breath. One non-functioning lung created intense labor to breathe, and the thought of running was a pipe dream.

The day wore on and the game progressed. Another at bat got me out at first, but the third took me all the way home with the help of my teammates who battled with purpose. The time after the game was rewarding, getting to know these locals who found great pleasure in playing and spending time together. The afternoon advanced with volleyball, attacked in the same manner as softball, with nothing to show for our efforts but bragging rights. Answering an ad in a local tabloid had been the best decision I had made since the one that brought me to this beautiful island.

Nothing in this league was taken seriously. We were known as the *bird league.* Each team was named after a different bird, whose name was artfully printed on each of our uniform T-shirts. The shirts were sometimes wild colors, mostly bright, and the comedy persisted with the fact that the director, Mike, who picked all the shirts and the printing colors, was color-blind, a fact that revealed itself years later. The lighthearted attitude led to comradery on and off the field. It certainly helped in getting to know people in this new community. The beneficial part was getting to know the families. All the kids were welcome, and everyone took care of them. It was a nice outing for parents, and for a registration fee of $20 a season, no one ever paid for a babysitter.

As time went on, the day came when I felt I belonged, as one of the *keiki* (children) crawled up in my lap to show me a great treasure she had found and called me "Aunty." I felt I had found my true *ohana* (family), and they were as acceptant and supportive as anyone could desire, without any idea of what I had been through in the past.

When I think back now, that was the beginning of a new life. Twenty years later I was still running the bases every Sunday, *talking story* and enjoying *puu puu* (finger food) after the game, joining in celebrations at their homes, and making the kind of friends that last a lifetime.

Through the years I continued thirsting for high and outside, slowed my speed down using heavier bats (much to the disbelief of the men), and enjoyed the spirit of the game, as well as the teasing I got for swinging at the first pitch. They found out I wasn't so fragile and began trusting me with plays. They were pleased and never realized how great that run between bases was for me.

Support is something that everyone needs, and whether I played on the Owls, Wrens, or Kiwis, I always felt my teammates were there for me, a feeling I would have relished in times past. Our end-of-season parties were days of families playing silly softball games, horseshoes, volleyball, and anything else we could think of to include kids and adults. The food was plentiful and so *ono* (good). Drinking of beer went on but never excessively, and in the rare instance that someone got carried away, there was always a designated driver. The beautiful thing was how everyone took care of everyone else. The aloha spirit was alive and well, and disagreements came and went like the trade winds. A band was present to add to the interactions. Everyone danced with everyone—something rare on the mainland.

My son came to watch at times, and my daughter joined the league in later years. Even my students came to check out this odd occurrence of *old* people playing softball. Twelve teams made up the league, so with six games played, we each played one other team on Sunday. No one on our team practiced, although some did on other teams, but no one could be too serious. When I would strike out and apologize, my good friend Nate would say, "There's no place for sorry in a fun league." Men like him were great to be around, and he was my best cheerleader. I would have given anything to have enjoyed that kind of support in years gone by.

This aloha spirit that I have been blessed with has surely strengthened my faith, but even so, glimmers of doubt rise up now and then as my mind recaptures the past. For even though I could run the bases with ease, use the bat with strength, and assist my teammates in winning, there was always that invasive memory that made me wonder if I was only *safe at first*.

CHAPTER 2

Coming Up Short

Looking back at the tougher times, I realized that overcoming obstacles is a way of life. We all go through this and for me, it seemed to be never ending. My life with my husband had brought me my dream of becoming a horsewoman and having a horse ranch. We had a custom-built home, two kids, two dogs, two cats, and two horses to start. With our newly acquired stud and our first baby on the ground, I felt that God had given me everything I had hoped for. Then, things got ugly.

My husband, a paramedic, was injured on the job, and the fire department disputed his injuries, refusing to pay him. My salary alone was not enough to support us, so we decided to sell the ranch and move up north where living expenses were cheaper. I would come to understand later that cheaper isn't always better. The emotional toll it put on my husband was more than he could stand. I was offered a transfer up north with my company, and I took it because not only was it infrequently offered, it supplied overtime which would create some freedom from the bills. I could stay at my in-laws' so there would be no living expenses, while my husband stayed behind to sell the house.

The strain of never being a paramedic again and feeling useless around the ranch took our temporary separation into oblivion. The battle raged on with the city, and finally, my letters got to the right people resulting in his being given a lifetime pension and health insurance along with a lump sum for back pay. Our kids stayed with him for the first year, until I found my life settled down a bit by finding a place to live with a trustworthy babysitter right next door.

Once my kids were back with me, my ex-husband remarried and had two more kids, and normality showed its face. I was settled in my job with new friends, my kids doing well in school, and even a boyfriend for myself. It seemed that my life was back on track. Without any support financially from my ex, we were struggling, but life was feasible. The clash came when my boyfriend only got to see his two kids once a year, and I had mine with me daily. On top of that, my health was declining. I chalked it up to overwork and stress. The doctor in Fresno told me that I just had the flu and gave me a vitamin shot.

Later, when I had my taxes done in LA, I went to see my old doctor. He was concerned, gave me a prescription, and told me to come back and see him if it didn't pass in a month. Busy mothers seldom worry about themselves, especially when they are single moms. Besides, I had faith that God would provide me with the strength I needed to carry on. As someone said, "If you want to give God a laugh, tell Him your plan."

After more problems on the home front and clashes over kids, I requested a transfer with my company and moved back to LA. New Year weekend was the weekend we had to find an apartment. We searched reluctantly but relentlessly experienced no success. The town of Northridge, where we were looking, was a college town, so several places were resistant to kids. I know the law says you can't discriminate, but guess what? Then, because it was Sunday and we hadn't been to Mass, I told the kids we needed to at least make a visit and begged them to pray that we would find an apartment.

As we left the church and drove around the corner, there was a vacancy sign. Having had refusals because of children, it was the first question I asked. The answer to our prayers—yes—and yes to a nice apartment, close to work, school, and shopping. The following weekend, we were unloading the car and our friend's truck and attempting to get settled. Everything was in a rush—apartment to organize, kids to school, and me to a new workplace. Things were coming together; even our church, where we had given our needs to God, was within walking distance, something I would come to feel was impossible.

Life continued. My daughter graduated from middle school and my son from elementary. She would join the drill team, and he would try soccer. I began working a second job as a waitress at the local diner to make ends meet. Before long, we became close to the building managers, and they were very helpful with my kids, something that would serve its purpose as God intended. This solidified my belief that God sends angels in many forms.

Life went on, and the kids seemed to adjust for the most part. My daughter had some difficulties fitting in. Even though her friends were quite obliging, I was not in the financial situation to compete with basically upper-class parents with two jobs. It's like the little Dutch boy, with his finger in the dike—one false move and it's all over. I tried as much as I could to fulfill her desires, even to the tune of a couple hundred dollars so she could participate in the Miss America Coed Pageant that she had been nominated for due to her Barbizon days in Fresno. Stresses mounted and although I never stopped believing God was in our court, it took its toll physically. Unsurmountable pressure came when my company started talking possible moves to Mohave and Oregon. Neither place appealed to me and the thought of moving my kids again was overwhelming. It also brought up difficulties of taking the kids out of state, which I was sure my ex would oppose.

The company's alternative was to take an early retirement. The offer that was presented sounded pretty good: one week of regular pay for each year served, plus vacation pay and medical pay for six months. This meant I would receive eighteen weeks of regular paychecks along with $1,200 to take training for another career. Trust me, fifteen years of phone company gives you experience in nothing much. The mention of designing trunks and arranging assignments at B-Boxes left a blank face on interviewers. Job integrity and organizational skills were all I could offer, but those characteristics were expected.

We've all heard that saying, "If it sounds too good to be true, it usually is." You guessed it; this turned out to be a perfect example. Instead of regular paychecks, we were issued lump sums to get us off the payroll by December 31. This was in September. After questioning our payroll who said, "Well, we've never done this before," we went back to the union and all they came up with was the company had agreed. My hatred for unions went into overdrive.

Still working for a few more weeks, I remember sitting at my desk, taking a service call, when I satisfied an itch under my arm and realized a chilling sensation when my fingers gravitated to a lump the size of a golf ball. Suddenly, the world was out of focus. Every scenario flashed before me. If it was cancer, this job was coming to an end, my insurance would only last six months, and who would take care of my kids?

The customer spoke, and I was back to reality. Taking care of the customer was first and foremost. As the day wore on, the future was hurricane rising. Driving home, the numbness took over. Lying to oneself was temporary relief, but I knew that the inevitable doctor's appointment was lurking. *God help me* was all I could think.

A few weeks later, the words the manager had said at my restaurant interview struck me. He said such a *slight* woman like me working with horses was hard to fathom. Now, as I got out of the shower, I jumped at the sight of a strange figure standing in the doorway. Coming to the realization that the figure, who looked like an eighty-year-old woman with skin hanging on bones, was me, convinced me to make the call.

It was Christmastime and the restaurant had put out its schedule where no one without extensive seniority was to have the day off. While I looked over the schedule, I noticed that the newest waitress had Christmas and Christmas Eve off. Spurred by my recent anxiety, I quit, deciding to follow my fears that this would be my last Christmas with my family. I packed up the kids, jumped in the car and began the five-hundred-mile trip from LA to San Geronimo, north of San Francisco, to my mom's. That Christmas, my brother and his family had come from Massachusetts, and my mom and stepdad rounded out the celebration. After a few days with my family, it was time to return home where God's plan was waiting.

The nursing staff that I knew so well was as pleasant as ever. Walking into my doctor's office, the telltale look on his face sent chills up my spine. The thing I always admired about my doctor was his honesty, but a part of me suddenly wanted to hear lies. His medical assistant, also his wife, was in the office, and he asked her for concurrence when I admitted my fears of breast cancer, rationalizing that one of my breasts was larger and harder than the other. When I first discovered it, my children's welfare crossed my mind, but also the chance of a future relationship haunted me. I was still in debt from my divorce, I had two kids, and I didn't even have a full-time job. Add to that being disfigured and I would be growing old alone. "My dearest Lord, what were you thinking?"

As the doctor ordered a full battery of tests, my fears lessened. He had always made me feel comfortable and cared for. I left the office thinking things were being handled.

Once home, normal routines took over, and dinner was on the table when the phone rang. It was Dr. Dane, and he wanted me in the hospital the next afternoon. When I told him I had two kids, the response was, "I know, I delivered them."

He continued by telling me he didn't care if he had to babysit them, I was to be in the hospital for a biopsy. *Biopsy*, a usually frightening word, seemed mundane as I went through the motions to arrange for my kids to be picked up (my landlord opted to keep an eye on them) by my friends (second family). I had lived with the Hollingers when I left home at nineteen, and they had always been there for me, just as they were at this life-changing stage of my well-being.

CHAPTER 3

You Gotta Laugh!

They say that laughter is good medicine. Well, it was in certain situations. Going through the details of that fate-filled day was matter-of-fact, and all was set for my kids to have breakfast after I left and wait to be picked up by the Hollingers sometime in the late morning. It was arranged that I would drive myself to the hospital and one of the family would pick up my car and take it to their house. Flashes of the future kept crossing my mind as I drove the twenty miles to the hospital. Because of freeways, twenty miles isn't much in LA, but as my fingers gripped the steering wheel, the miles took their toll.

Checking in at the hospital was routine for them, which increased my anxiety due to lack of personal interaction. More blood tests and X-rays brought me to my room with its sterile atmosphere and that antiseptic smell that goes with the territory. Without my kids I felt like a fish out of water, laying in the not-so-comfortable bed with nothing to do but think about tomorrow's surgery.

My mind was saturated with my overactive imagination's response to the numerous *what-ifs* that I digested. Just when I wanted to get up and run out, in came Mom Hollinger and her daughter, Julie, to rescue me from the battles of my mind and take possession of my car for safekeeping. Having gone a year without a car, it was foremost on my mind with the fear of being towed or stolen. It was a relief knowing my treasure would be guarded, but without that worry, my mind was able to slip into the fears of surgical concerns.

Even though my real family was absent, the comfort given by these two ladies brought me peace. Mom H talked of remembering me in her prayers that night and the next day and scolded me for not yet having called my mom. With a promise that I would, Mom H and Julie left for home where my kids were busy being fed and readied for bed by the rest of the family.

A nurse arrived shortly after a call from my doctor who confessed that he didn't know how I was still standing with so little blood. He told me he had ordered transfusions before my surgery could occur, and the nurse had arrived to exact the plan. As the IV started, I watched the blood travel slowly from the bag that dangled above me attached to my bed into my arm where the needle invaded my vein. Laying quietly for a half hour or more, it necessitated my secret time with God.

Various thoughts and questions crossed my mind, and I knew there was only One with all the answers. Asking what the results of the biopsy would be didn't bring an immediate response, but the fear eased as time elapsed. I simply prayed thanking God for giving me the strength and courage I needed to face the future. Looking toward the bag that dangled next to me, it was as if my fears drifted away as did the blood.

As I creased the bedsheets with a bit more ease, the nurse arrived to replace the bag with another. Chatting about kids and work, she added to my calm. Just as she was finishing, she flipped the bag, splattering me, the bed, the bed rails, sheets, and pillow with blood. Quickly grabbing the bag before more damage could be done, she apologized profusely as she tried to wipe up the blood. Running out of the room for cleaning devices, the nurse left me briefly, lending me time to begin using tissues to wipe some of the blood spatters. Returning with towels and new sheets, she was mortified saying, "That was such a rookie mistake." She explained that she had left the plug out before flipping the bag.

I looked around at the blood-painted scene and began laughing. "This looks like a crime scene or horror movie," I relinquished.

With that, even she couldn't hold back the laughter. She proceeded to change the bedding, my gown, and all parts affected as we continued our amused banter. Thanking me for my understanding, I told her she certainly took my mind off my surgery, which brought another round of laughter. As we've often been told, "God works in mysterious ways." This reiterated the necessity of laughter in times of trouble and fear. One of my favorite pictures is of the laughing Jesus. It reminds me He has a sense of humor.

There were also those times when things got so ridiculous that all I could do was laugh, sometimes breaking into uncontrollable giggles to the point of tears. From dropping cereal all over the floor watching the Cheerios roll in every direction due to lack of strength in my hands to allowing my daughter to make numerous piglet tails out of my hair, the intenseness of the situation demanded any outlet that did the job.

My son, who was ten and very protective, and I would watch silly movies together, like *Smokey and the Bandit* and *Cannonball Run*, especially the outtakes, which kept us laughing and our minds diverted. During that time, Burt Reynolds became the hero for myself and my son. His antics with Dom De Louise were great distracters from the truth. Comedy is valid medicine when threatened with life-changing experiences. Other TV comedies aided our escape from the monster that lurked in the sidelines.

One time when I went for treatment, the nurse sat me down to take my blood for testing and was startled when she saw the end of my finger. She noticed how many prick marks there were and instantly said, "Did I do that?"

I just laughed and told her that I had been hemming a dress, and no, I never use a thimble. It just doesn't work for me. In any case, we both got a good laugh out of it. It's important to give credit to the oncology nurses who always seem to be upbeat. That refreshing attitude is advantageous to healing.

Money being tight, my kids and I luckily had the TV and a few movies recorded on VCR tapes (yes, old school). Various comedies, the funnier the better, were a good deterrent to the grim thoughts, and the kids needed distraction from such adult complications in life.

CHAPTER 4

God Sends Angels

We all would like to think that we are self-sufficient and can work through life without any help. However, God has destined us to be subjected to a wonderful barrage of angels that come in all shapes and sizes, bent on making life bearable.

One of my greatest faults was never asking for help. No matter how tough life's troubles were, I chose to struggle through on my own rather than wound my pride and ask someone to lend a hand. Faced with single parenthood with no support, I simply worked two or more jobs, never considering the consequences I would have to face with my health and my children.

From the day I decided to leave Fresno, I began encountering angels. The first was Billy, always a good friend, but in this instance the answer to my silent prayer, not knowing how I would get all my belongings and two kids into my Camaro—like putting toothpaste back into the tube. Decked out with a small trailer behind his truck, we managed to take full advantage of this angel with our move to Northridge.

After becoming established with the new job and the kids in school, we seemed to be on our way, starting a new life. Just when you think you've figured out God's plan, He throws you a curve, but He also provides angels to get you through it. Taking the early retirement seemed a light at the end of the tunnel, until the phone company and the union got together and decided to get everyone off the books by the end of the year, lumping all monies together. Having had my future destroyed, it seemed unreal when sitting at work (with only another week before retirement), feeling the lump under my left arm. Disbelief coursed over me as a flash of uncertainty came to life and the fear of my children's future.

Despite my dysfunctional relatives, the family I had lived with when I left home were my merciful angels, not only caring for my kids, but giving them a family of love at a time when their world was in such upheaval. Fear can overtake children in different ways, so being able to be in the company of such loving people was comforting to both, especially my son who took everything to heart. Paul was the ultimate father that the kids were drawn to. He was funny, loving, strict, and empathetic. As an LAPD officer for many years, he was the epitome of strength and virtue. Mom H was the heart of the family, the lioness who protected all her children, of which I was blessed to be considered one. After my surgery, she made sure I was well taken care of for a few days and finally released me to go home.

Recovery from the biopsy, which had revealed Hodgkin's, was brief, when a second band of angels came into my life. On an uneventful evening a few days after hearing the news, the phone rang to redirect my future. The oncologist, whom my doctor had recommended, was demanding my presence at the Northridge Medical Center that evening. Up until this call my strength had gotten me through, but because the Hollingers were out of town and I was basically on my own, I intruded on the managers of the apartment complex. Knocking on their door, I burst into tears, stating in a muffled manner the demands that had been placed on me. I admitted that I didn't know what to do with my kids. As angels often do, Dolores turned to her husband and said, "We can take the kids to the lake with us, right?"

His answer was "Sure."

Like I said, angels come in all facets of life. These two appeared at the opportune moment, making me think back to that fateful day when God led us to His choice of apartments. Dolores took me to the hospital, getting me settled for the tests which would commence early in the morning. Although fear of the findings was bouncing around in my head, there was a peace afforded to me with the realization that my children were safe and in good hands.

While undergoing the many tests that were scheduled, a special woman, who was a volunteer, entered our lives. She comforted me in between tests and arranged for people in my church to bring food (completely prepared) for myself and my kids after I returned from the hospital and throughout my treatment. She had told me that she wasn't a member of my church but was a member of an ecumenical choir of which my church was part. The angelic inclusion of Nadina came in the form of transportation for my kids to school activities when my treatment took its toll and visitations at my apartment making me feel less alone.

Nadina worked for Universal Studios which initiated a special request that triggered an over-the-top response. My son and I had seen *Indiana Jones: Raiders of the Lost Ark* at a special showing when we went to the movies for his birthday. From that time on, he was an avid fan. One day when we went to In-N-Out Burger, they were running a promotion for the movie, and he got a glass with his meal. Weeks later, after one of my treatments, he was in his room looking very depressed. His first reaction to my inquiry was that nothing was wrong. But knowing my son, I kept pushing and the tears began to flow as he admitted that he had clipped the edge of his precious glass on the faucet, causing it to shatter. My comfort had minimal effect, but the Holy Spirit instilled wisdom, and I made the call since the promotion had ended. Within a couple of days, Nadina showed up without the glass, but with enough Indiana paraphernalia to appease a dozen boys. In later years I came to wonder if the glass meant so much because it connected to something he and I had done together, and his fears told him it might be the last. In recent years, I sent him the editor's book on the movie as well as the pewter tie tack, which he was pleased to receive. Nadina continued to be a bright light in our lives for years to come.

Someone who skirted on the belief of being an agnostic became a member of the angel brigade. Rich, the boyfriend I had left behind knowing I couldn't work and guessing my financial situation, took it on himself (with a little encouragement from the Holy Spirit) to contact various people I had known and worked with to gather donations on my behalf. The much-needed funds arrived at a point of desperation that did my heart good. Months later in our conversation, he experienced some difficulty in believing that the Holy Spirit had anything to do with it. After a while, his mind was more open to the possibility. God works wonders despite his reluctant workers.

Amid the turmoil of treatment, God sent His angels to my doorstep. I got to know the generous spirit of the people in my church and in my apartment complex. Everyone was gracious, never condescending, and always cheerful. One of the effects of this disease that really bothered me was not being able to attend Mass and receive the Holy Eucharist. One day my prayers were answered when a woman from the parish arrived at my door carrying the Precious Gift. I have no doubt that this added supplement resulted in the rapid escalations of the abilities of the drugs that were being pumped into my veins and gave me strength to endure them. I remember repeatedly how my oncologist would walk around me shaking his head and saying, "Very gratifying, very gratifying."

At one point I apologized, "I don't mean to insult your beliefs, but my mother has the world praying for me."

His response was, "In your case, I'll take all the help I can get."

Numerous messengers from God came into the mix of things from the women in my Renew group to my older brother who offered his home as a refuge during my treatment, including calls of encouragement from friends and family. The Healing of Memories conference that the Renew group took me to cleansed old wounds that generated internal healing. Moving to North Carolina with my brother was an option, but one, when prayed about, exposed the necessity of continuing my treatment with Dr. Singerman, who had been introduced by my physician Dr. Dane, as one of the top oncologists in the nation. Trusting that God had sent me to the right doctors, the best city, and the most effective medical center, I opted to decline the latter offer, while also considering the problem of taking the kids out of state.

I've come to realize that throughout our lives, God sends messages and messengers to guide us, but we don't always listen or learn.

It reminds me of the story of the man trapped in his house through a flood. He watched the water rise and prayed for help from God. Before long, a motorboat came along and yelled for him to jump on, but the man refused. He kept praying for help as the water continued to take over his house, so he climbed to the second story. Once again, a boat came along calling for him to join them, but again he refused. Finally, the man climbed to his roof and waited and prayed, and a third boat came along offering to save him, but still the man declined.

As he prayed, the water overtook him, and he drowned. Once in Heaven, the man talked to God about what had happened. He asked why God had ignored his prayers, and God said, "I sent you three boats and you refused them."

I often think back on how many times I must have ignored God's saving grace, but with this cancer I began to see the light, so to speak. My own rendition of the child's catechetical response to "Where is God? God is everywhere" is that God isn't necessarily in every situation physically but makes sure He sends the right people to be there for us. They don't always respond positively either, but He is always with us no matter what, in one form or another.

CHAPTER 5

Degradation

I have tried, over the years, to describe what cancer was like, and the closest I have come is rape. Cancer destroys your well-being, negates your natural abilities, upsets your livelihood, misshapes your family, and redirects your life. It is fearful, chaotic, rebellious, fracturing, destructive, and degrading. Many people associate cancer with lack of hair, vomiting, and loss of weight. Although true, these minimize the real effects.

From the very first visit to the doctor in Fresno, I felt ignored with the lack of concern I received. This doctor did not so much as touch the enlarged glands in my throat that I complained about. His *Coverdale cocktail* as he referred to it, was effective for approximately twenty-four hours, at which time my incessant coughing resumed. Had I stayed in Fresno at the hands of this supposed healer, I most likely would not be writing this today. It never hurts to get a second opinion. Some people might attribute my bloodbath in the hospital as degrading, but as I explained, it was a positive distraction.

Once in any hospital preparing for surgery, the rush is on to prepare the patient and as much as possible protect their privacy. When being given drugs that make you loopy, your mind begins a multitude of emotions: fear, sadness, uncertainty, and degradation, among others. There is the concern that in the company of doctors and nurses, they have seen it all, so it's not definite that they are concerned with modesty. The underlying thought that a surgeon that you do not even know is going to be cutting into your body to extract a once viable part of the glandular system that has gone rogue is difficult to ignore. Once out of surgery, there are any number of nurses checking on your incision, your water intake, and your ability to eliminate.

Reintroduced to more tests at the medical center, the degradation continued. From dawn to dusk and through the early evening, I was subjected to prodding and probing by any number of staff. One that stuck in my mind was an enema that was given by a male nurse (believe me, I have no prejudice against male nurses) who, to my embarrassed revelation, had left the curtain around my bed, which was by the exit door, partially open for all the world to see.

More tests meant more *revealing* as the days progressed. When a doctor came into my room with the announcement that he was there to take a bone marrow sample, I was not too alarmed. He asked me what my doctor had told me, and when I explained, "There would be a lot of pressure," he said, "He lied."

Pressure was not the problem; it was the pain that they could not numb because the bone had to be excavated to procure a sample. I am not a person who easily demonstrates pain or discomfort, so it was degrading to be lying with my butt exposed, screaming into a pillow while the probe invaded my bone. Just as I felt the agony subside, an apology erupted. When I answered the question "What is it you're here for?" with "Hodgkin's," it was painfully revealed that the sample retrieved was too small. At that point, I just wanted to disappear, but the pain brought me back to reality. Because of the location of my bed, I am sure that I entertained the thoughts of more than one person as to what was being done behind that curtain. I had been through childbirth twice and would have opted for a third rather than another bone marrow test.

Another day, I was taken to radiology where I was given an enema of trace material while being fed a glob-like substance that caused me to gag. It was embarrassing enough being fed and probed by two male technicians while obviously clothed with nothing but a hospital gown, let alone using every ounce of fortitude to keep from vomiting or eliminating literally in the faces of my attackers.

More tests brought about increased discomfort and revealed embarrassment. There was a substance I was fed on an empty stomach that had to migrate to a specific place in my digestive system. This procedure, although painless at first, began in the early afternoon or early evening. Time and again I was wheeled down to radiology just to be told, "No go."

When finally it was a go, the procedure took less than a half hour, and the pain of my starvation was about to end. Because I had missed the regular meal schedule, a wonderful nurse procured a luscious sandwich, with chips, pudding, and milk. Every bite invaded my taste buds with great appreciation. While relishing the last of my tasty meal, apparently the oncologist had seen all he needed to see and ordered an extra potent serving of chemo drugs. The injection was nothing crucial, until the after affects emerged. It was as if something was ripping me apart. The degradation comes when you realize that the horseshoe-shaped pan they propose for vomiting doesn't even come close. My fingers could not reach the nurse's button fast enough to avoid erupting onto surrounding territories. As the nurse came in, her words promoted the obvious. "You really are sick."

In a matter-of-fact manner, she handed me the washbasin while taking away the other and vowing to clean me up. I spent years holding heads, restricting hair, and comforting kids during bouts of flu, but being on the receiving end violated my personal worth. Once the embarrassment was over, I could not help but think about all that delicious food that hadn't had a chance to embed itself.

After leaving the hospital, I was able to drive myself to and from chemo treatments without difficulty initially. Once the drugs began dissolving the cancer, symptoms appeared more readily, and the drive resulted in less than comfortable results. On one occasion I had to pull over to throw up, and it ended up in the car. It mortified me that my thirteen-year-old daughter was cleaning up my mess. Other times I was ashamed to ask her help when my fever peaked, and I needed ice packs and cold compresses on my legs, head, and arms. As the chemo continued, my weakness progressed and even walking down the hall to the laundry room was a task. My son took over the laundry and even found enjoyment in cooking. Not being able to work and support my kids, do the laundry or cook or even drive much or attend Mass made me feel inadequate as a mother and a person. After all, a mother is supposed to take care of her children, not the other way around.

In trying to support my children and stay in our apartment, I investigated the option of welfare. After meeting with the agent and answering all his questions, along with all the insinuations he made, mostly regarding my car, I felt violated. I had known people on welfare that didn't go through this much scrutiny, but I felt it necessary for the sake of my kids. Weeks into interrogation and investigation of our home and personal possessions and property, I once again found myself in a weakened state, sitting in front of the agent who pronounced that since I had been working, I didn't qualify for welfare or food stamps. He suggested that I apply for state disability. That day our cupboards were bare, but God always provides, and our neighbors were obliging. A few days later I was granted an emergency draft until my regular state checks would be issued. Once they arrived, we could at least eat. Almost half of the check went to pay for medication, but at least it was something.

Not being able to keep up with my bills was devastating, especially my car payments. Unfortunately, I didn't remember an insurance policy that protected me in times of unemployment or illness. I begged and pleaded to make interest-only payments, and of course was allowed, but not one associate at the credit union that I had been with for years ever noticed the policy, regardless of the fact that I was making the premiums. After fifteen years of financing cars and personal loans on time and even with early payoffs, they talked to me as if I was a deadbeat. Stress over bills did nothing to help my condition, knowing full well that stress is the bottom line of all cancers. Feeling useless and like a failure does nothing but wear on the mind and the body.

During the time of my chemo treatments, tragedy hit our family when my stepfather was struck with a heart attack, sending him into the hospital debilitated by coma. My faith was tested once again when I begged God to spare him, knowing how much my mother needed him. We don't always understand God's plan, but Tom was taken from us without warning. After the funeral and time spent with my mom, I returned to my chemo treatments which became more and more invasive and sometimes were delayed when my blood counts plummeted. We know that God works in strange ways, and looking back, it may have been his way of interceding in my family's plight.

Months later, my mom was sorting through Tom's possessions and figuring discernment for those things left behind. My mom, allowed to stay in the house for as long as she needed according to Tom's will, was given leave to disperse his personal possessions according to her discretion. Because I could no longer afford my car payments, I offered to buy Tom's older model car, so I could sell my car before it was repossessed. My mom opted to sell his car to my sister's boyfriend rather than her own daughter. Degraded to the point of being less important than a nonrelative, I hoped that I could return to work soon and catch up on my car payments.

Toward the end of my treatments, it would only take a matter of minutes before I became sick. The reality of it is the less cancer there is to attack, the more that the good cells and organs are targeted. Never knowing exactly what the reaction would be, it was hard to be prepared. On one occasion my insides were so disruptive that I did not know which end was destined for the toilet. Laying on the bathroom floor, panic set in as I noticed blood in the bowl. Barely able to reach the phone on my nightstand (we didn't have the cell phones of today), I finally managed to drag it to me and call my landlady. Cautiously explaining my situation, I told her I needed to call my doctor but could not reach my phone book. Within minutes she was at my door ringing the doorbell, followed by, "Oh, shit!"

Realizing she had forgotten her key, she soon returned to find me on the bathroom floor. Although it was an embarrassing situation, all I could feel for the moment was relief. A call to my doctor and Dolores's husband Paul was off to the pharmacy to pick up a prescription for Coke syrup. Within minutes of swallowing, my insides began to settle down. The doctor explained the blood as broken blood vessels from excessive vomiting, which should repair themselves shortly. Despite the degrading situation, these angels of mercy had come to my rescue.

When your body fails you, your emotional makeup, courage, and strength are quick to follow. Just as older people need that purpose to get up each morning, so, too, someone being debilitated by cancer repeatedly feels insecure in self-worth. Even though my children were my drive to keep fighting, there were times when even God had difficulty giving me the inspiration to carry on. However, God never gives up, and while I wallowed in self-pity, He never faltered in making His presence known.

CHAPTER 6

Learning to Fight

Attitude is half the battle of fighting cancer. Developing the right attitude can be difficult if you've never learned to fight for yourself. Growing up in an abusive environment makes way for timid reactions to challenges. Subtlety is not an option when it comes to cancer. The word *cancer* itself scares most people, and fear can be a deadly weapon.

I can still picture my doctor standing at the end of my bed when I woke up from surgery. His poker face didn't reflect anything as I waited anxiously to hear what treatment was available to fight breast cancer. His opening statement was, "There's good news and bad news."

My response was, "Get to the good news, and we'll skip the bad news."

He half smiled and said, "There are two types of cancer that we can cure, uterine and Hodgkin's. You've got Hodgkin's."

Relieved that I didn't have breast cancer, I waited for the bad news. He told me that it was curable when caught at stage 2, but I had developed into stage 4. He directed me to an oncologist in Northridge who practiced at the medical center down the street from my apartment. At that point I'm not sure how much fight was in me.

They say you can't give what you don't have. Most of my life I don't remember anyone fighting for me. I do remember when I was in fifth grade and my teacher gave me a *C* in art. I've always been good at art. My grandfather was a professional artist and taught me things from the time I was little. My mom went to talk with the teacher who told her that I didn't deserve the *C*, but she didn't want it to look bad by having too many students on the honor roll. She said it didn't matter because it was only art. My grandfather, as a professional, was livid, but was told not to make trouble by my mother. It stung even more when the awards for honor roll were presented and the other fifth grade had seven students, and my teacher only had two, her favorite two.

In high school, when girls had to wait for boys to ask when prom came up, everyone thought a certain boy would ask me, but he was talked into asking another girl by my best friend. She had told me once that there was no such thing as friendship where a boy was concerned. I figured out by her actions that she meant it and was saving him for herself, at some later date. She presently had a boyfriend but wasn't ready to get serious. I felt sorry for him.

At the end of my junior year, I wanted to go into the two-year nursing program at the junior college, which was affiliated with Marin General, the best hospital in the area. My mom met together with the dean of girls and decided I wouldn't make it in nursing because I wasn't a good math student. They decided that I couldn't possibly do well at chemistry, even though I was good at lab biology and physiology, a college course that I had opted to take instead of another study hall.

After high school, when working full time while trying to carry a full fifteen-credit schedule at the junior college, I realized that I was maintaining a low B average without studying. This made me plan on other options that would get me into the workforce. I wanted to become a flight attendant, but my mom and a friend of the family decided it wasn't right for me because "Stewardesses are short-lived" or so the friend thought. They talked me into taking a supermarket course, and right after graduating from the six-week course, the markets went on strike. Another detour seemed to be at hand. My aunt had worked for the phone company for years, so I made my own plan to apply for a job, and a classmate's father worked for them and put in a good word. I wanted to work for a year and save my money so I could go back to school without working full time. The best laid plans, as they say, and fifteen years later, I was retiring from the phone company.

The closest I got to someone fighting for me was when I planned to leave home, and Paul wrote a letter to my dad telling him that he could take care of any problems that I might encounter. He will always have a special place in my heart as the father figure I never had. If I had spent more time living with his family, I might have learned to fight, as I watched Paul fight for his daughters in various incidents. He was a defender of his girls, all five of them.

I've been reminded of a movie with Meg Ryan called *You've Got Mail*, in which she tells her email buddy that she was always frustrated with herself because she could never think of those fighting words to say in any given situation. My empathy was in full gear hearing that because I had gone through that exact frustration. Hours, days, weeks, even months after a conflicting instance, I would regret all the choice words, phrases, or even full speeches that I wished I had thought to voice but failed behind the wall where cowards go to hide.

When I got married, I assumed that my husband would defend me. Never assume. One evening when we were at my parents, my dad, in his drunken stupor, came marching down the hall calling me a liar. My husband, knowing it wasn't true, never said a word. Later that night, my husband Joe, couldn't understand why I was so upset. It hurts even more when someone you love betrays you.

Some people you grow close to at work can also be painful. Even though I was always good at what I did for work, I just did my job, and if I didn't get recognition for it, that was okay. It did irritate me at times when other people got credit for my ideas, but I was usually just happy that the job got done. Learning to stand up for oneself takes training, and that doesn't always come easily or quickly.

Often in my present employment I have been chastised for not following Matthew 18. There are times when I want so much to say what I really think—to say how I've been hurt by someone, but years of feeling that I have no right to defend myself has taken its toll. My ability to hold my temper and back off has been my best weapon in life. I have two rules that I have stuck by over the years: I don't go where I'm not invited, and I don't stay where I'm not wanted. It has worked well for me, but it has also cost me. It doesn't do any good to keep those disturbing instances inside. Cancer thrives on such anxiety. Matthew had it right. It's good to face your problems and level with those who cause discomfort. The world would be a much more peaceful place if we could all be so honest. Knowing this, I still need some work in this area.

My failings in the sight of battle have cost me several victories, which of course distresses me at a later date. Various instances of landlords that cheated me, employers breaking labor laws, even personal advances that I walked away from instead of fighting have left me plagued most of my life. Taking the initiative to do anything, even writing this book, is a struggle for me. I'm getting better at speaking up because my excellent memory haunts me. Should of, would of, could of is where I find myself in a whirlpool. I should have fought harder with my credit union when they wouldn't honor my insurance. I would have been better off if I hadn't taken the early retirement. I could have fought for my contract renewal. All of these are spilt milk, and I as well as others need to learn to let it go and let God.

With all the baggage I brought with me, the one thing that helped was that I wasn't fighting for me. From the very beginning, I was fighting for my kids. Fear of them ending up with their dad was a motivator. He had a new wife and kids, so I knew it would be a hardship for us. God and I had conversations about this. I told God how unfair it would be to lose their mother after losing their father to divorce. When Joe divorced me, he divorced our kids as well. What I got in response to my protest was a command to fight. As tired and weak as I was at times, it wasn't easy—in fact, near impossible.

When I lost my taste, it almost drove me crazy after getting over the initial shock. To hear that it was normal was not a big help. I had some angry words for God when the mad cravings, because of lack of taste, woke me up in the middle of the night. When you can't taste anything, your mind plays tricks on you, telling you it's starving. This is not just craving pickles and ice cream when you're pregnant; this is cravings on steroids. Minimal relief came with cheap white bread (we really couldn't afford the good stuff anyway) lathered with creamy peanut butter. It wasn't a cure-all, but it certainly gave temporary satisfaction. This is the big problem. When you can't taste, you don't feel like eating; when you don't eat, you lose your strength; when you lose your strength, you can't fight; when you stop fighting, you lose the battle.

CHAPTER 7

Different Strokes

Introducing the idea of cancer to your kids is not that easy, and the way they handle the news is not necessarily equal. Although boys and girls see things differently, personalities add more to the equation. My son wouldn't leave my side. I had to chase him out of the apartment to get him to go play with his friends; my daughter was business as usual.

There always seemed to be that fear of losing for him. Although the divorce hit my daughter harder, my son was more affected by the cancer. He would sit in the living room working with his Legos and then explain his creations to me. To this day, my son has been my protector.

My daughter was a different story. Her way of handling it was to be in denial. She would go to school and all her regular activities as if I were just like I'd always been. She arranged for me to take her and her friends to drill team practice on my treatment days and various other things. She expected me at her games and set up inconveniences no matter how I was feeling. Getting her to help with her brother, according to her calculations, was asking too much. She always needed something for school despite the fact that she knew money was tight. It was her way of pretending it was not happening.

People react differently for their own reasons. I went to visit a friend of mine, a former coworker, and we had what I thought was a nice visit. We had some snacks and talked about the difference of working in Fresno versus Orange. I found out the latest gossip from the phone company office, and I helped her with the laundry and finally told her about the chemo I was going through. She seemed to take it well and mentioned that one of the other ladies we had worked with had been diagnosed with cancer. Sharon and I had been the best of friends working together in Orange. Because I transferred to Fresno, Sharon had gotten the next promotion, a position I knew she was more than qualified for. After leaving that day, I sent letters, cards, and even called, but never got an answer. I remember even apologizing if I had scared her, but still I never heard from her.

Reactions vary with different circumstances and relatives are no exception. When I returned to my mom's after my stepfather's funeral, I was over at my stepbrother's, and his little girl, who had previously stayed distant, was coming up to me. She was so cute and wanted a drink from my Coke, so I turned the glass so she wouldn't be drinking where I had and gave her a sip. My stepbrother's wife, Dori, came around the corner and practically freaked out when she saw what I was doing. I just looked at her, but to myself, I wanted to say, "Cancer isn't contagious."

She made an excuse that she didn't want her to have soda, but I had seen her drinking out of her dad's soda just minutes before. Some people just have strange ideas. I had kids ask me if I was contagious. It brought about a better understanding of how people with AIDS felt. Coincidentally, the type of cancer I contracted is related to the immune system, which makes me ineligible to donate blood, something I have always wanted to achieve. I have told the blood bank volunteers since that they should want my blood because I beat stage 4 cancer, so it should be extra powerful blood. They cease to see my sense of humor.

The night I was in the hospital for my biopsy, I did call my mom, but the response I received was less than supportive. Months later she admitted that Mom H had called her, telling her that she needed to come to be with me. My mom justified her lack of movement saying that she had a job and couldn't just pick up and leave. I knew the priest she worked for and under the circumstances, he would have let her go in a heartbeat. My stepfather would have put her on a plane as soon as possible. She told me later that when she got off the phone with me, she burst into tears, but at the time, all I felt was abandoned.

Once treatment was over and I wanted to get back to work, companies were resistant to hire me because I told the truth about the year I was off work. After being rejected time and again, my confidence bottomed out, and the future looked bleak. My mother's prayer petitions to everyone she knew had gotten me through the chemo, and my prayers to the Holy Spirit inspired me. From that time on I filled in the gap with *freelance writing*. When asked why I didn't continue, my response was that it wasn't lucrative. Lying is not a good thing, but sometimes desperate times call for desperate measures. It wasn't a complete lie because writing has always been my comfort at times, escape at others. During my bout with cancer, I journaled, but of course it wasn't for sale. Maybe this is my reprieve. Once my new methods went into action, I landed a job at Hickory Farms as an assistant manager. Because no one knew me and had no idea what I'd been through, I was home free.

One evening the phone rang, and thinking it was one of my daughter's friends calling after nine o'clock, I answered rather abruptly. A voice from the past responded after a brief hesitation, and I was speechless. Michael and I hadn't spoken in twenty years, but the feelings hadn't evaporated. We talked for hours beginning with his confessions that had he known of my illness, he would have been with me. We arranged to meet at a Denny's in Newhall to where he could catch a ride from a coworker. As I drove there after work, my hands were sweaty, my stomach queasy, and I felt like a teenager again. Waiting for him to show up was nerve-racking, and then the moment arrived. He stepped out of the car and before I knew it, I was in his arms, and that first kiss was like our first kiss twenty years before. We talked, he met my kids, I met his, and time flew by with laughter, good times, and attending church together. I felt alive and loved. Our kids got along together, and the world was a better place.

Months later, Michael came with me to my mom's for Mother's Day, and she was thrilled. She had loved Michael since we were teenagers, and the happy situation brought joy to everyone. My kids were enjoying the visit, and while I was in the shower, Michael and my daughter disappeared. Coming out of the shower, my long, wet hair wrapped in a towel, I was met by Michael who grabbed me by the hand and dragged me out of the house. Bare feet are common in Hawaii but not in Northern California. We drove to the spot of our first date where he proceeded to ask me to marry him. It was to be a new beginning, or so I thought.

I moved myself and my kids back to Fresno, which my landlord thought a bad idea due to my contracting cancer after only two years during my former habitation. My old company was offering better wages for contract workers, and Michael was living not far away in Visalia. Sitting at Mass one Sunday, I heard the sermon about love, making me realize then the extent of my love for him. When you are willing to put your life on the line for someone, that's true love. Although a proven point, it isn't always reciprocal.

The only way I could move was to farm out my kids which was very difficult but necessary. My daughter went to stay with my mom, which gave her some company with Tom gone, and my son went to live with Rich, my former boyfriend who had gotten custody of his kids. I rented a room from a friend who also worked for the phone company. She was not only a good friend but became one of God's angels when my son crashed his bike and she invited him to come stay with us while checking on a possible concussion. Agnes offered continued support as time went on.

We had planned to go up to my mom's for Christmas, and I had asked Michael to go with us. When my son crashed his bike, I had to stay up all night checking on him, which was going to make it difficult to stay awake on a three-hundred-mile drive. Michael's devotion began to be questioned, as he borrowed money to buy his family gifts and then refused to drive my car to my mom's. Later, thinking about it, I wondered if God had allowed my son to get hurt to open my eyes to Michael. Our Christmas with my mom was bittersweet. We were with family, but it suggested the thoughts that crossed my mind the year before, when I had prophesied it being our last Christmas together. What I didn't understand was that the missing person would be Tom.

As months passed, my engagement seemed to falter, and little by little, Michael's unfaithfulness began to raise its ugly head. Disbelief kept my hopes alive partly because he and my son had made such a connection. It was gratifying to have a manly influence for him. Periodically, God was sending messages of warning, but my prayers that Michael would come around resulted in negative responses. I will believe until the day I die that God meant Michael and I to be together, but God only makes the plans, and He allows us to make the choices, right or wrong. Michael made his choice, and I was forced to make another when the job I had fell through with the phone company's decision to close the office, ending my employment.

One evening, as I was talking to Agnes, my roommate, I saw my car being towed away. The credit union had decided to repossess my Camaro. Without a job or a car, the future was dim. Fresno had minimal public transportation. I took a bus to the bank one day, which was about two miles from my house, which took me two hours. God does work in mysterious ways, as the lack of a car and job and the necessity to be out of Michael's reach led me to the decision to move to Hawaii, where I could get around without a car. I knew their bus system was one of the best. As the Bible tells us, God provides for the birds; why wouldn't He provide for us?

It took me awhile to understand Michael's actions. He was a guy with a lot of baggage, and someone running from his mother's curse. On her deathbed, she had told him to never have another woman in his life, and then she died; he was only seventeen. He knew I had gotten over cancer, but because I hadn't passed that five-year safe zone, he couldn't take the chance of losing me too. He just couldn't handle the possibility, and in his mind, it was probably the sign that his mother was still in charge, and there would be no woman in his life except her. As heartbreaking as it was, I listened to Fr. MacGregor, a priest friend who had known both of us as kids, who told me, "You can't help someone who doesn't want to be helped."

People who knew me in California, except Agnes, seemed to look at me waiting for my nose to turn colors and fall off. I began to understand how the lepers of Hawaii felt. My mother showed everyone pictures of what I looked like before chemo. They were horrible pictures that solidified the need to fear my collapse at any moment. Moving to Hawaii represented freedom from peering eyes and stereotypical attitudes about cancer. I was looking forward to joining new communities and experiencing different strokes for different folks.

CHAPTER 8

Feeling It

Emotions ran the gamut while surviving cancer. Fear of not being able to raise my children was foremost; in fact, it brought about the only favor I asked of God. My fervent petition was that God would allow me to live long enough to see my children, who were ten and thirteen at the time, grow up. God has blessed me tenfold by gracing me with grandchildren and great-grandchildren. However, throughout my chemo, I had my doubts and questioned God.

As I lay on the living room floor due to back pain I could not handle, I was forced to entreat my daughter to massage my cramping muscles. It made me feel demanding and worthless, having to depend on the children with whom I once played ball in the park, took to the beach, enjoyed occasions to Disneyland, and engaged with trips. I felt the annoyance from my daughter as she placed the cold compresses on my arms and legs to bring my temperature down. I understood the discontent in my kids when there was not enough money to buy food or go anywhere. Mothers are expected to be strong, vibrant, knowledgeable, talented people who juggle all the household tasks with one hand while planning the future with the other. Unfortunately, at this time of life, I was none of the above.

Anger came frothing from my mouth when I could not accomplish simple tasks when needed. My upset with my kids flared up time and again when it should have been focused on myself. One night I was so frustrated that I pulled out a suitcase and started packing my clothes, screaming at the kids that I was through trying because they did not understand what I was going through. My son ran out of the apartment and adeptly brought back Dolores, who calmed me and held me in her arms as I sobbed in frustration and embarrassment. That was only one of the low points of emotional stability.

Feeling alone is different than being lonely, drawing from the depths of one's soul. It sets you up for failure while it ravages your heart. Being alone, while the world is coming down around you, is painful enough, but feeling that way when two children depend on you is devastating. They were my reason for wanting to live, but no matter how many hugs I got from my son, being alone was still gaining ground. Cancer puts you in a category that divides you from the normal population. When my insides were being ripped apart, I could not share that with anyone. My family sent notes and made occasional calls but always from a distance. Alone brings out fear, emptiness, frustration, desperation, and longing.

When I was married, the one thing I ate up was my big strong husband wrapping me in his arms, making the world go away. No matter what had gone wrong, who unnerved me at work, or how frustrating the drive home was, Joe could make it all vanish, creating an enormous fortress of safety. At this time of being alone, I missed that feeling and longed for someone's protective arms around me.

My belief in God's presence dwindled at these times of abandonment from the world. Thoughts of dying crossed my mind, as I wrote in my journal, "If I died, who would care?" I had been to various funerals and seen avenues of cars in procession, chapels bursting at the seams, and an abundance of floral tribute embellishing the fragrance of the air, but I could pathetically picture the empty seats in the case of my demise. There probably would be some attendance from those respectful of other members of the family. Even my dad's celebration of life, which I felt was a misnomer, packed the church with religious, bridge officers (my dad worked on the Golden Gate Bridge), friends from church who were so close to my mom, and other family friends.

Of course, my stepdad Tom's funeral was magnanimous with representatives from the police, the navy (for my brothers, both naval recruits), the religious, and numerous family and friends. In contrast, Tom was a loving, joyful man who relished life, whereas my dad was forever miserable, but both procured respectable consideration at their funerals. Contrary to them, my state of mind evolved into an empty chapel sporadically peppered with a few close friends, minimal family members (some with their crocodile tears), and my brother officiating. My son would probably be the hardest hit. Other than that, I had no reason to believe that there would be any great interest in my passing.

The cancer had attacked my confidence, creating an instability in any future plans. All dreams or goals I harbored were diminished by the disease. That desire to go on, most probably designed by the Holy Spirit, evaporated like the setting sun, as the torment of poisons elevated into unbearable measures. It was an ongoing battle to keep my spirits up for the sake of my kids. My place of refuge had been taken away, as I realized the limitations of my body no longer capable of withstanding the necessities of attending Mass. The church had always been my place of comfort through an abusive father, a cheating husband, divorce, alienation from family members, financial difficulties, and job displacement; now this, which seemed to be the straw that broke the camel's back. Where was God in all this? Had He abandoned me as well? That aspect of being alone haunted me.

As I mentioned before, my writing had always been a way of escape from pain or discomfort. Writing poetry requires the attention of emotions with no inhibitions. It is a place where the writer can go and feel free to express their innermost, soul-searching feelings and frustrations. The following is a poem I recently ran across that I wrote during those terribly draining times:

Shadows That Follow

Though death should dare to show its face
Among the summer sun and haze,

Life brightly glimmers dawn 'til dusk,
With hope that makes "Survive" a must.

Though weak the body, strength comes through,
Avoiding death's unwanted shrew.

Fear filters in, at dark of night,
And shatters hope that dulls the flight.

For children's sake the fight goes on
Dispatching threats, "Disease be gone!"

In meekest times, God must be cursed
When chemicals dish out their worst.

No more the body is one's own
Besieged by devils once unknown.

The cure becomes too much to bear,
Creating feelings of despair.

About the time strengths slide and break,
Docs revel at strides treatments take.

Light reappears, though shadows wait
While life goes on unknown is fate.

by Pamela M. 1985

There were some high points that brought a smile to my face or caused a blurting out of emotion. When I first started chemo, the oncologist warned me of the loss of my hair, describing it as clumps suddenly falling out in the shower. My mother also feared the loss of my then waist-length hair and verbalized it whenever she talked to me on the phone. One more caution from the doctor and I burst out in frustration, "Between you and my mom, what is it with you? My hair is not the thing I'm concerned with."

The oncologist apologized saying he just wanted me to be prepared. My apology for the outburst followed with the explanation that my greatest concern was survival, not hair. The hair issue became laughable when I realized that my head was spared (God's favor for my mom), but all the rest of my hair had gone away. The amusement came with the realization that it was a heck of a way to keep from having to shave my legs all the time. When I thought about it, it provided a snicker.

Lasting thoughts of prior holidays rekindled some sense of hope that each holiday that elapsed would not be the last. While others were stressing over the upcoming holidays, I was smiling at the thought of spending one more Christmas with my kids.

One afternoon in between treatments, I was upset by my son's disappearance on his bike. He finally showed up to tell me he had lost the key to his bike lock, which left it prisoner at the store. Weak but urged on by adrenalin, I went down with bolt cutters from my landlord to free the captive bike. After returning home with anger brewing, my son approached with a card in his hand, admitting that he had gone to the store to get me a card to make me feel better. Tears came to my eyes as I held him in my arms with a smile in my heart for this precious gift that God had given me years before.

Feelings and emotions were like the chemo drugs, shooting off the chart or coming to a calming end. Pregnant women often experience the evolution of moods and reactions. Chemo is pregnancy to the max, never giving warning as to what to expect next. The two are parallel in that they deliver the gift of life at the end, at least that is the preferred outcome. Then, fear takes over wondering "What if?" and conjuring all the elements or circumstances that could go wrong. My trust in God's goodness wavered through pregnancy as well as throughout chemo. Somehow, when I had my head in the toilet bowl, I hoped God was not watching any more than I would have wanted either of my earthly fathers to see me in that condition.

When the ninth month of chemo ended and I went in for my final scans (minus the bone marrow test, which I adamantly refused), I was ecstatic about gaining my results. Dr. Singerman was pleased, and just as I breathed a sigh of relief, my calm was shattered. Because of two areas that were still somewhat enlarged, he wanted me to go through one more series of chemo, which included three times a week for another month. I left the office fractured, ending up sitting in church asking God, "Why?"

We often hear that God only sends us as much as we can handle. I am sure I am not the only one that feels that to be questionable. This last element was too much. I was out of money, still unemployed and unable to look for work, having difficulty with the kids and their frustration of wanting to get on with a normal life, and patience had become foreign to my vocabulary. Life, loosely translated, had met its Waterloo. Four more weeks of torture, not just for me but for my children and for the neighbors and friends who had come to our aid. All my strength, independence, and self-sufficiency had been challenged, leaving me struggling through all the emotions that were devouring my existence.

CHAPTER 9

Signs

We have all heard people say, "It's a sign," and believe it or not, it sticks in the back of our minds. Although some *signs* are in the recesses of our imagination, there are those that we should sit up and take notice of. Signs come in all sizes, colors, and images. When you wake up having had a very vivid dream, it just may be a message from God. Even so, it needs to be analyzed for what it is, without adding our human frailties. Being honest with yourself is first and foremost to understanding the signs.

When only a few weeks went by after getting the supposed all-healing "cocktail," I was once again coughing up blood, which I should have reacted to sooner. We get distracted by outside forces, such as children, significant others, and work. It was easier to just stick to the daily routine than to concern myself with personal health.

Relationships come with their own signs. Control, jealousy, demands, and selfish needs all pointed toward domestic abuse. It was the furthest thing from my mind when one night during an argument, my arms were seized, and I was thrown against the wall. Ladies, fear leads men in relationships, fear of loss. They usually don't have the strongest self-confidence, and when they involve themselves with an attractive partner, their imagination goes wild, and they believe that there is no reason for them to be the primary focus. Men are just men, not evil beings for the most part—just human, with human fears. We all fear loss; I feared the loss of my kids. That's why

I ignored many of the signs that were evident relating to my failing health.

The experts agreed that I contracted cancer about two and a half years after being in the central valley. Environment is one of the factors of Hodgkin's, as well as stress. Of course, having gone through the destruction of my marriage, I was not ready to accept that I could once again be losing at another relationship. The final sign came one night when I had run to the store for some missing dinner items, only to come back to my boyfriend bragging about how he had spanked my son. I was furious, not because of the action, but of how proud this 280-pound, six-foot-two-inch bully was to attack this little ten-year-old boy. Before threatening the bully, I ran to my son who told me he was okay. Shortly after, I put a transfer in with the phone company to return to LA. Looking back, I think that last sign came from God. Once in LA, no man was allowed in my house as a protective measure for my children.

Michael was the only exception. Even he came with signs. Did you ever love someone so much that you created excuses for every fault and any infractions of human decency? Despite the fact that I was still recovering from chemo, I busied myself with helping him move, settling in his new house, and loaning him my car, which he returned with a bent rim. I began wondering about his loyalties, and when he refused to drive with us to my mom's, I wondered how much he cared, knowing I was exhausted from staying awake with my son all night checking for a concussion. The signs were all there, and finally God implanted the thought that Michael would always be able to manipulate me, providing I was close enough. After my car was repossessed, it was clear that God had another plan for me and my kids.

While undergoing chemo, God was already directing me toward his eventual plan. As humans, we want instantaneous results, but *God's time* is not necessarily immediate. As Fr. Hamsche had told us at the healing seminar, God's miracles are usually not sudden. They come to be in God's time, when He knows it is right for us. If my insurance had continued, I would never have had the opportunity to follow the sign and put my trust in God.

My weakness, loss of weight, and inability to talk for more than a few minutes without coughing extensively were all signs that I ignored before I was diagnosed, but they were also signs of my healing which I almost missed. I remember a conversation with my younger brother on the phone one evening, when one of those signs came to fruition. After talking for a while, my brother noticed that I had not coughed in about a half hour. Most people need physical signs to believe. Remember how Thomas wouldn't believe until he put his fingers into Christ's wounds? Many times, we taunt God with the same demands.

It may sound strange, but my fingernails have always signified one of those signs. When my nails do not split and break but grow out, I know my health is good. Did you know that circulation can be checked on your fingernails? Push down close to the quick and see how fast the white returns to pink. It is a simple thing to do to help believe you're headed for good health. During chemo and before, my nails broke and split and were so weak that they broke as soon as I tried to use them for anything. While chemo saturated me, I didn't notice at first, but they improved, and since then have proven to be my billboard for health.

The upside of losing my body hair was not having to shave my legs or underarms, so the sign that things were returning to normal came with the daunting chore on a regular basis. It became a welcome task rather than a thankless one knowing it meant healing. Even if I had lost the hair on my head, the sign would have come that healing was happening because God counts every hair that you lose and replaces each to recreate the perfect temple He has devised. I believe He also takes care of those who experience the loss and cannot handle it. My mom would have been devastated, and I am sure He knew that.

The first time I noticed my loss of taste was trying to enjoy a popsicle. There were other food items that had just not tasted as good, but I chalked it up to the meds and not being very enthused about eating. But you know the vibrant taste popsicles have and I could not taste anything. The peanut butter on white bread became the only thing I could taste, so when I bit into a piece of fried chicken and the tasty, crispy texture settled deeply on my tongue, I realized the healing quality of God's love.

As I mentioned before, men are led by fear, and I should have seen the signs in Michael with his lack of commitment. Having lost his mother at seventeen, I am sure in the back of his mind he was fearful that it was hazardous territory to give his love to another woman who might die and leave him. Not only was this the attitude with Michael, but it existed for a lot of the people in my California communities. The fact that people seemed to be anticipating my destruction or demise seemed a definite sign that I should *get out of town*, so to speak. A new beginning away from familiar medical facilities and anyone who knew my history was evident.

A year after I was in Hawaii, upon the return trip from California, I experienced another sign. As the plane descended over Pearl Harbor and the wheels touched the runway, the enveloping feeling came across me of "It's good to be home."

CHAPTER 10

Abandoned

For years I heard stories about celebrities who underwent battles with various types of cancer. The first one I can remember was Patricia Neal who battled cancer and won if I remember correctly. Family, friends, and fans boosted her spirits and health as she went through her ordeal. Others came into the news being touted for such bravery for sharing their challenges with the world. There was a positive aspect that created an awareness among the general public, resulting in lives being saved. It also gave strength to the celebrities, a kind of strength that revels the human need for closeness and companionship. When I was in high school, our choral group sang "No Man Is an Island," and the meaning of the song is personified by the wellness that came about for those celebrities as they were saturated by love and concern.

Cancer is hard enough to battle without having to do it alone. The noncelebrities soon lose the camaraderie that attacks in the beginning. People swarm and it is wonderful, but they seem to lose interest when treatment appears to be doing its job. I frequently thought about those celebrities, thinking how they would battle without all the attention. I hope they were sincerely grateful for all the blessings they received, but once the fanfare was over, were they able to survive?

A few of God's angels like the Hollingers, my older brother, my landlords, and Nadina continued their support, but others considered their responsibilities over. This attitude of mine may sound ungrateful, however, it is a natural response to that sudden loss of attention. Michael's sudden charge on his white horse was exhilarating at first. When you've been through an illness that makes you experience total loss, it's a refreshing change when someone rushes in to rescue you. Loving someone so deeply is God-driven. After all, His command, "Love one another as I have loved you" is a hard act to follow. I came as close as I could with Michael, but when he went his own way, the abandonment set in hard.

Coming to Hawaii was a struggle. At times I worked three part-time jobs with a full-time position. From the second year, I played softball which kept me connected somewhat. The local people lived by the aloha spirit. When you hear all the stories of them growing up together it makes you envious. That guilty feeling that emerges wears at the gut and may come around to bite you. Things went wrong by leaving my daughter on the mainland, even though she chose to stay. But you cannot undo the things that are done. Life is like a rolling snowball that gathers momentum as it rolls, while tacking on experiences as it rotates. I missed out on certain occasions, like my son's AIT graduation, and events while trying to survive financially, and I wouldn't blame either of my kids if they felt abandoned. It is a lonely existence that was never purposeful.

Cancer does not just last for the duration of the actual disease. The aftermath comes at you like the recurring waves of the ocean, some large, some small. Society continues to turn its back as the big *C* evolves as a fearful giant that labels you as fractured, unfit for normalcy. The experiences that drove me from California were the shadows that followed me to Hawaii and made me certain that my mainland secrets needed to stay there.

Even though I did not share my secret, knowing what I had gone through lowered my self-confidence. The cancer continued to work its damaging effects as it kept me from feeling free to get involved with anyone. Those in my softball league assisted in building my confidence, but since I was not anywhere near that coveted *five-year* mark, there was always a feeling of insecurity knowing that technically, I was not cured. Wanting to find financial security for my kids made me long for life insurance, which had abandoned me when I could not continue my premiums. Before cancer, I was in possession of two life insurance policies of more than fifteen years, one private, the one that I purchased at nineteen when I first started working at the phone company. The other was through the phone company.

Prior to leaving Fresno, an agent had talked me into modifying my policy from $7,000 to $10,000 with the promise that my equity would pay the premiums on the new policy for two years. Questioning the status of my policy, I was told the agent no longer worked for them, and the inability to pay my premiums would result in cancellation. Even though the premiums were around $25, that was enough to feed my kids for a week. At that point there was nothing to do but give it to God. What was required immediately was more important than that which might be needed in the future, which, God willing, wouldn't be until after my kids were grown. For my sake, or to take care of my funeral expenses, if necessary, God would have to stay with me past that *five-year* point to bypass the stringent criteria.

Cancer is debilitating physically but also destructive of confidence, stability, and strength. Abandonment by companions, family, friends, employers, and society comes with the territory. My refuge was in the knowledge that no matter the challenge, God would be there to guide me through. He never promised that life would be easy, but He did assure us that He would be there for each of us to help us endure. As it says in my *Jesus Calling* book, "Trust is the channel through which My Peace flows into you. Thankfulness lifts you up above your circumstances."

CHAPTER 11

Resolutions

In the beginning, my resolve was to survive for the sake of my kids. This kept me going through thick and thin, a lot of times more thin than thick, but always there along with my on-again, off-again faith in God's abilities. I realized that in order to get upset with someone, you have to believe in them because it is the trust we put in them that is tarnished when things don't go the way *we* planned. God certainly doesn't need our approval for His plan, but we continue to question and let our feelings run amok.

After the chemo had ended and my attempts at jobs had failed, I began to see life differently. Even with all the hurdles and pitfalls, along with my decision to start over in another state, my faith helped me find a sense out of chaos and confusion. All my adult life I had always opted to be within driving distance of my mom, but this new move would negate that possibility. In the past, after my dad died, it was necessary to be close enough to help her clean out her creek, which consisted of overgrown blackberries intermingled with poison oak, salvage the basement when it flooded, and finally move her to San Rafael, leaving behind sad and happy memories to start life anew.

Once my chemo concluded, my doctor released me after begging me to have the tests over again, but my insurance had expired and even though I went back to the company and the union, both refused to extend my insurance regardless of the fact that I was paying the premiums. After being in the Renew group from church, I concluded that it was time for me to accept my healing and move on. I believed and still do that if I hadn't been healed, my insurance would have continued so I could take the tests, but it was time for me to put my trust in God, who always provides our needs. As they say, "There's no such thing as a coincidence, just God being inconspicuous."

Another chance to understand God's plan was when I went on an interview for General Telephone, the competitor for Pacific Telephone where I had been working. The interview went well, and all I needed was to pass the physical. My doctor had filled out his part of the report and the GTE doctor kept asking me questions about weakness and dizziness, which I gave a negative response to. When I read both reports, I called my doctor. He had been mistaken thinking it was paperwork to continue my state disability, so I could take another week or two to get acclimated. When I talked to him, he apologized saying he would make it right. I knew he would get into trouble, which he passed off as workable. Even so I could not do that to the man who had saved my life. After much consideration and alternate plans, I realized that God must have seen things differently.

There are often signs that we sometimes overlook because God can be extremely subtle. I remember the day that the doctor told me he wanted another round of chemo. I felt like the rug had been pulled out from under me. When I walked into the church feeling lost and empty, I poured out my heart to God. I never felt so alone, but without warning, I felt that gentle, warm hand on my shoulder, and a calm came over me. From that time, my belief in my healing and my future seemed evident.

A dream I had at nineteen had collapsed in front of me when Michael retreated from his promise to love me forever. He had left me in those early years and again twenty years later. Believe me, the essence of "Fool me once shame on you, fool me twice shame on me" passed through my mind, and forgiving myself for being made a fool of erupted like a violent storm. Finally, seeing things from a different perspective opened my mind. Seeing Michael after so many years revealed that we had an extensive amount of catching up to do and were astonished to find that we had lived parallel lives. God had placed us in the same vicinity from before we met at my brother's school. I will believe until the day I die that God meant Michael and me to be together, but unfortunately, we don't always follow His plan.

When I decided to come to Hawaii, everyone said I was crazy—that I would get *rock fever* and long for the mainland. This decision was not made lightly. I considered where I could live in a place my kids would have a good life and I could use public transportation. My need to get away from people who looked upon me with pity or fear was foremost. It was also necessary to get far enough away from Michael where he could not control me. I asked my friends not to divulge my whereabouts because I didn't want to spend my time looking over my shoulder. I saw Hawaii as a new life of freedom from various anchors.

My brother had lived in Hawaii and had arranged for some contacts when I got here because I had no place to live and no job, which was a bit unnerving. A friend of my brother's had secured a place for me to stay at the Cathedral Convent in Nuuanu where a few nuns were staying for the summer. They were so kind and supportive in my search for employment. One interviewer asked me for a contact number and when I told the manager it would be answered "Cathedral Convent," he asked if that was where I was staying; and when I said "Yes," he said, "You're hired." That was my first part-time job. At one point I had three.

I was limited to area because of bus transportation, but I managed. When my son came to join me, he stayed at the convent, too, until we found a place. The nuns were so good with him. He was thirteen, small, but acceptant of change, never complaining. We managed to move using the bus, and he got started at school. Because he knew money was tight, he arranged to go to school early every morning at five thirty to work in the cafeteria, so he could get free lunch. It pained me to see him go to those limits because I could not provide. Once I had three part-time jobs, I rarely saw my son, and the depression began to take its toll.

One day, before my son arrived, while looking for full-time employment, I went for a ride on the bus the long way to Kailua and stopped at Hanauma Bay. It was so beautiful, which seemed to raise my spirits, but as I walked to the edge of one of the high areas, the sound of the crashing surf caught my attention. The water invaded the shore leaving no crevice spared as it gained energy to retreat into the arms of the awaiting sea. Almost mesmerized by the sight, I began thinking how easy it would be to start running down the slope with no ability to stop. As if a force came over me, my feet slipped on the loose lava rock, causing me a quick sit down. Stunned, I sat listening to the surf, but this time the waves seemed cleansing and refreshing, wiping away any vile thoughts of ending anything; instead, I was overwhelmed by a sense of guilt knowing how ungrateful my actions would have been.

My daughter had opted to stay in San Rafael with my mom in order for her to finish her senior year of school. I had agreed and on the way to the airport, I gave her my engagement ring from Michael, telling her that he had given it to a seventeen-year-old girl, not a thirty-year-old woman. She was expected to come to Hawaii after graduation but got sidetracked by a guy who made her promises.

I had rented a house big enough for the three of us, but my finances alone, even though I had secured a full-time job to go with the other three, was not enough to keep us there. Because I was in a lease, even after we moved out, the landlord demanded I pay the remaining months. Again, my inability to fight for myself took its toll. I could have fought it if I'd had the time because she rented it to the military right after us. Unfortunately, greed is the root of all evils and often throws unfair punches. Perhaps if I had known how to fight for myself, I could have kept her from taking such advantage.

We rented a room in an apartment with a single mom of a two-year-old. Because she never cleaned her kitchen except the day we first saw the place, I bought frozen dinners for my son, so he could use the microwave and then eat in our room with our silverware. When I came home one night and found my son upset, he admitted that he had been saving the veal parmigiana, and she had eaten it. When my tips that I kept in a jar started disappearing, I began looking for another place. Having to use the toilet at the pool time and again because her daughter kept throwing things that didn't flush in the toilet at the apartment was bad enough, but when I found out my son was skipping school because of bullying, it was time to move on. After doing some research, we found a place in Kailua with two bedrooms and a bathroom with a young man whose parents had bought the house and moved to the mainland. Finding out that my son was doing well and liking school was music to my ears.

In my attempt to check all the boxes before coming to Hawaii, I had written a letter to my ex-husband that I needed him to sign. Because we used the same lawyer (big mistake) for our divorce, I was under the misconception at the time that my ex had to have custody because the kids were going to stay with him in the beginning. He had family around where he was living, and I was working excessive hours to pay bills, as he was only working minimally due to his back injury. Even though my son was thirteen and able to choose where he wanted to live, I still needed a sign off for medical care in an emergency. He sent back my letter with a note saying, "Before any emergency treatment, I am to be notified." Furious and frustrated, I called child services to explain the situation, and the representative asked how long the kids had been living with me. When I told him seven years, he told me I had de facto custody and was free to take my son wherever I needed to move. As I said earlier, I was always able and willing to fight for my kids.

Because of this incident, when another problem arose, my *always-by-the-law* attitude went out the window. My son, who had never complained, worked to save me money, was never in fights, an active youth leader at church, and was so excited to get his license had been told he had to produce my divorce papers before he could get his license. Knowing full well that if we had to get his dad's permission it would be the same fiasco as the medical agreement, I called the driver license division and asked what I needed as proof if my husband was deceased. As far as my kids and myself were concerned, he was dead. He had never paid child support or helped with any of the kids' expenses, and from the time he got remarried, our kids came last. When they told me just my word, I told my son not to say anything, and he proceeded to take the test. The officer was complimentary about his driving, and my son went home with his license. I was determined that my son was not going to suffer because of anyone's stupidity or vindictive attitude.

When we lived on the mainland, after the divorce we moved several times based on employment and living necessities. Coming to Hawaii, I promised my son that he would be in the same high school for four years, and barring the first unfortunate semester, the promise was fulfilled, and he graduated from Kailua High School. Shortly after, he joined the army as a reservist and twenty years later, he is still married to the military.

My daughter had come to Hawaii for a couple of years. She was never happy with her life in Hawaii. She had come to the islands with a daughter, who was a toddler, and left the islands with my granddaughter and grandson years later. She moved to Colorado, which she found more suitable.

Coming to Hawaii, I resolved myself to stay far away from Michael, and after dating a few different guys over several years, I resigned myself to living alone. There was one man who at the baseball park tugged at my heart, just as Michael had done years before. Even though we played on the same team, I cooperated in his custody battle for his son and was appreciated for helping him quit smoking; we remained friends. This revelation came as he made it clear that I was not in his league. He was the only man that had ever made me feel the way Michael had. So after that, I resolved to concentrate on work and my horse.

I did question God time and again as to why He taught me to love so deeply but never gave me anyone on which to use that ability. Of course, after thinking about it, I realized that God had sent two such men, and I had loved them with every ounce of my being, but they had chosen to follow their own path, not God's. There is a story I use in my guidance class that I believe goes hand in hand with God's command.

It seems that Oscar Hammerstein, the great composer, had handed a small note to Mary Martin, a devoted actress, when they were working on Broadway before her performance. It simply but powerfully said:

> A bell's not a bell 'til you ring it
> A song's not a song 'til you sing it
> Love in your heart wasn't put there to stay
> Love isn't love 'til you give it away.

This was the last thing he ever wrote, and Mary Martin treasured it as I have because it reminds me that God never promised the return of love except from Him.

Every New Year, people make resolutions that they break within days, sometimes hours, and they run the gamut from losing weight to taking their first cruise, even though they fear the sea. Getting over fears has got to be one of the resolutions that people desire but avoid.

One of my fears was going places alone. I enjoyed the baseball league because we did things as a team. After twenty years, some old-timers left the team, but most stuck around. The guy I had such deep feelings for had quit. I think he began to feel like I did, being left out of get-togethers and parties. I usually found out about pot-lucks the day of and get-togethers the day after, so I neglected to sign up again for the twenty-first year. God had led me to this league where I had made friends and enjoyed being out on the beautiful Hawaiian Sundays, and He had given me many years of joy. To leave the Kiwis, which took me ten years to get placed on, was difficult, but it was certainly time to move on.

Another part of my life that brought me to acquaint myself with new people was when I bought my horse. It had torn my heart apart to lose my horses with the divorce. "Never say never," as they say. A vendor I worked with asked me to find him a horse, and since one of my customers at the restaurant (one of my part-time jobs) was always asking me to come see his ranch, God led me to meet and get to know an old *paniolo* (cowboy), Martin Knott. He helped all kinds of people, loved family, and stood by his wife even after she became incapacitated with Alzheimer's. He left this world at ninety-six headed straight for the pearly gates. I am sure God was waiting with open arms for both of the Knotts.

Martin sold me a way of life. From the very beginning, Iniki, named Merlin at birth, was the love of my life. He had my attention twice a day every day. I fed him morning and night, cleaned his stall, and exercised him. We spent pleasant times together, and I was introduced to a new world of companions. In Hawaii, there are long lines of families who participate in various horse events and rodeos. Even in California, I found horse people to be good people, willing to help one another. Horses, I believe, are God's tools that are effective in changing people, healing hearts, and comforting the lonely. Iniki was my friend, confidant, companion. A rescue horse from Kauai, he had rescued me, giving me purpose and soothing the void of being needed.

After twenty years at the same stable, I was forced to find a new stable due to small-minded people, but God led me to a place where everyone loved Iniki and helped him overcome the agitation he had developed with people trying their own methods on him when I wasn't around. He enjoyed a large turnout with a beautiful huge stall under roof. For two years he was loved and appreciated for the spirited animal that he was. Unforgiving rains saturated the ground, making it hard for even me to walk without sinking. It is not hard to figure that a 1,200-pound animal would sink even faster. There wasn't a dry spot in miles. I wheeled loads of gravel into his stall until the path became unpassable. Unable to reach a couple of my horse buddies, I prayed to God and put it in His hands.

Iniki was acting strange, but I was at a loss. Someone in my Renew group had told me that you do as much as you possibly can, and then give it up to God. I asked for His help but promised that I would accept His will. The next morning, a woman called me from the stable telling me he was propping himself on his front leg. When the vet came, she said he had damaged his nerves and had no feeling at all in his leg. She commented what a sweet boy he was, and I complied. With nothing left to do, I gave the order to put him down. It broke my heart, and I still miss him because I did not just lose my friend and companion, I lost a lifestyle and my purpose.

God always knows what He's doing, and in my case, the loss of Iniki, whom I was blessed with for twenty-two years, cut back my expenses in time to pay for extensive dental work that was necessary. Even though my teeth make me feel great and improve my health, Iniki still tugs at my heart. No one understands how horses become a part of you, unless they have been so blessed. I feel that God was generous in bringing Iniki into my life, but the emptiness that resulted is hard to ignore.

Since then, the idea of getting another horse has crossed my mind but quickly tossed aside especially since this newest health issue has emerged. Having paid out over $3,000 for office visits, tests, surgeries, and pathologies, I realized God's infinite wisdom. It pains me that Iniki, at twenty-six, could have lived another ten years, but to be ungrateful for losing him would be an insult to God. One day, before I'm too old (since Martin was in his nineties), I hope to be blessed again with another beautiful animal, who will never replace Iniki but will at least partially fill the void he left behind.

Probably the most important resolution I made was to refuse to let others change me to suit themselves. We should only be concerned with pleasing God, and we should satisfy our personal talents and gifts. We were created in the image of God, and although we can never attain His glory and goodness, we should strive to be the best self we can be. We have been graced with so many wonderful gifts and are expected to use them to their full extent. So many times my writing has been put on hold because of the opinions of others. Writers always talk about writer's block, but there is another kind, and that is when fear takes over because one or more of your "friends" or relatives tells you of their dissatisfaction or their own ideas about your story. This puts the writing on the shelf, once again. Resolutions are meant to help or improve a person, not weigh them down or punish them. The grace of God is there to help resolutions evolve, and He never means to hurt or deny anyone. If I've learned anything, it is to be true to myself, which pleases my Father.

CHAPTER 12

Here We Go Again

Cancer-free! Those are beautiful words that any cancer patient wants to hear. Once past the five-year mark, you are home free. Except when you go through chemotherapy, you learn that those effective poisons that pump through your veins actually do break down resistance to other cancers. So haunting the recesses of your mind is "What's next?"

Having passed through the five-year checkered flag, followed by ten, twenty, and thirty, expecting the caution flag to suddenly appear had evaded my thoughts. Visiting my cardiologist, he referred to a spot on my collarbone as something to check out. Thinking that the "age spot" had been there for at least six years caused me to escape any caution. Stepping out of the shower a few days later, my eyes were drawn to a spot I had ignored for years, about the size of a half dollar, suddenly exhibiting drastic modifications. The once mildly scattered brown coloring had metamorphosed into an evil, dark substance that demonstrated a nodule about the size of the head of a match. A sudden chill went down my back, and a force took over me to follow directions: "See a dermatologist."

Going through the computer to find a dermatologist close to work, accidents do happen. I read a bio that impressed me, and I called for an appointment, but it turned out that he was in a different location. As they say, and I've said before, there aren't coincidences, just God being inconspicuous. Having never been to a dermatologist, I arrived with so much speculation that my mind was in a turmoil. A few minutes into the meeting and I was at ease, except for the invasive questions of melanoma. The doctor demanded a rush on the biopsies he performed that day and suggested that I come in for a full body scan. His last request set the wheels turning, and my active imagination, along with my sense of modesty, erupted into thoughts of my naked, far-from-perfect body stretched out on a table for all the world to see. Fearing the worst, I almost cancelled.

As luck and the Holy Spirit would have it, my fears became manageable as I arrived at the office and was taken into the exam room. The nurse told me to take everything off, which froze me in my tracks, until she said, "You can leave your bra and panties on."

What a relief, and all the prior visions vanished. The doctor was extremely respectful, asking if I had any restraints on areas I felt too uncomfortable. For some reason, with this doctor, common sense took over, and the idea of a *full body scan* being restricted was stupid.

The procedure continued with pictures of moles and markings that were suspicious, eventually leading to ten biopsies. A little discomfort and several bandages later and the two-hour ordeal was over. He took the time to explain the next steps, showed me the pictures they had taken, and engaged the help of two nurses in the processes. Mentioning that the rules were that doctors could only be paid for three biopsies per visit seemed ludicrous. So if he had played by those rules, I would have had to return for at least three more visits to complete what we accomplished in one, meaning more cost for the patient. The question remains in my mind, *Who are the insurance companies there for?*

Accordingly, God sends angels in all forms. Within a couple of days, due to the rush that was imposed, approximately 50 percent of the biopsies were identified as cancerous, with only one being melanoma. The doctor called me after hours to relate the news, having refused to let the Thanksgiving weekend stand in his way. Scheduling of surgery followed; the basil on my face was an in-office action, but the melanoma demanded hospital efficiency due to the necessity of a special dye-initiated scan that would pinpoint the *hot spot* concerning the lymph nodes that were connected to the melanoma. Just the word *lymph node* sent tremors through me due to my earlier experience with Hodgkin's.

The day of surgery, my good friend dropped me off at the same-day surgery entrance, and it suddenly felt like I was on my own. I had read in my *Jesus Calling* book that morning which reminded me:

> Take time to be holy. The word holy does not mean goody-goody; it means set apart for sacred use. That is what those quiet moments in My presence are accomplished within you. As you focus your mind and heart on Me, you are being transformed: re-created into the one I designed you to be. This process requires blocks of time set aside for communion with me.

Due to my being *early* as everyone kept telling me, there were plenty of opportunities to be with God, and in the private times of waiting from one step to the next, I listened to His encouraging words.

Thanks to a wonderful nurse who was extremely helpful and loving (she even gave me a hug before surgery and one when I was going home), my time waiting for surgery was peaceful. When the surgeon came in, accompanied by the anesthesiologist and a young resident, he explained what would transpire, followed by a few words from the anesthesiologist. Shortly after, I was wheeled into the operating room. It struck me that the image we see on TV of huge sterile rooms with big lights and lots of people in attendance are seriously undercut by reality. The room was compact with a few nurses and doctors. My surgeon was sitting at a computer just inside the door, the young resident began adjusting my legs in order to attach leg massage boots, and a nurse told me she was going to apply a blood pressure cuff...then nothing.

I woke up back in the general room surrounded by curtains, with the same delightful nurse sitting at a computer, monitoring two of us post-surgery recipients. She kept telling me to breathe deeply, offered me a drink, and encouraged me to wake my body bit by bit (sitting up, going to the bathroom assisted by another nurse) and focus on any discomfort. I had arrived at 5:45 a.m. and by 2:30 p.m. I was headed home via my friend.

One week went by before the supposed fatal day when pathology reports would be revealed. Because my truck is rather large for the hospital garage, and partly because I didn't want to be alone, my friend drove me to the hospital. After being taken to the exam room, I kept thanking God for bringing me to this renowned surgeon. Of course, the weak side of my humanity suggested fear of the results of pathology. When the surgeon came in, he explained the ins and outs of the surgery and then left the room to check the pathology report. It broke the tension and made me laugh. He returned speaking the words that touched my heart, reviving my gratitude to God and bringing tears to my eyes as I expressed my relief and appreciation for his news. Clear of cancer once again.

The receptionist grabbed both my hands congratulating me. My friend had stepped out in the hall for a phone call. She hung up when she saw me, and her response to my news was with unbounded love exhibited by a hug that warmed my insides. We cried together on the way to the elevator and on the way back to school, I told her all that had happened and what was said. We got back just in time for me to join the other teachers for our Christmas luncheon. Only three administrators knew what had been going on. One by one I quietly told them the simple yet enormous results of "I'm clear." They agreed that this would be a great Christmas.

CHAPTER 13

Why Not Me?

Often in life, we confront the question of "Why me?" But there are also times when we look around and see people who we judge as less worthy who seem to have everything go their way. We sit back wondering what we've done wrong, or why it is that some people can do anything they like—never go to church, hardly know anything in the Bible, and treat others, including their families, like dirt—and yet seemingly have everything they want in life.

We've been bombarded throughout our lives with the promises: "Ask and you shall receive; seek and you shall find; knock and the door shall open." So when my cancer was flaring or I was looking for a job afterward, it was natural to look at others with wonder and some envy, but mainly with confusion. My question to God was, "Why me?"

Throughout the years, I always heard that God only sends or allows what you can handle. Well, let me tell you that I have argued with God about His perception of my strength. Of course, God always won that argument, letting me know that He had created me and groomed me through the years to have the strength of a bull and the courage of a lion. Even so, I still have my doubts (about me, not Him), but as I grow older, I just knuckle down and forge ahead with the assurance that He will be there when I need Him, or He will send one of His angels.

Being judgmental is unacceptable, but our humanity falls short of accepting that restriction. Be honest. Didn't you ever look at celebrities or sports figures and comment on the lack of balance of haves and have nots? It's natural to wonder what star they were born under or where they found the four-leaf clover that has guaranteed them the path to success. So where can we obtain these magical trinkets? We can't. Who knows why things work the way they do? Only God knows the reasoning of life, and someday we will, but for now, we need to trust that everything happens for a reason. Those things come from God, and they are for the best conclusions.

I am guilty of forgetting that concept when I experience the immoral actions of others or witness lying or stealing that is justified as "Everyone does it" or "It's a victimless crime." Believe me when I tell you that I've been tempted. Friends of mine, when I was getting over chemo, asked me to steal their mink coat out of their car on a given day and sell it. They would collect the insurance of $5,000, so it would end up a win-win situation. I declined, and within a month I heard from a mutual friend that the mink had been stolen.

Another time I was at the movies and met some people I knew. We were there to see the same movie and enjoyed it, but when it was over, they said they were going back in to see another movie, only having paid for one. This was someone I had a great deal of respect for, but no matter how much I tried to dismiss it, my mind returned to the fact that she was cheating or stealing. No matter how you look at it, it was wrong, and yet looking at their lives, they both have beautiful homes, families, and good jobs. Could I be doing something wrong? Is that the reason they succeed?

Early in my adult life, I was given the ultimate temptations. My boss, who was an attractive, charming man, offered me an apartment, car, bank account, and clothing if I would just be available to him. I heard about another girl whom he had set up the same way, and she had enjoyed it but decided to move on. At first, I thought he was joking, but having been assured he was not, being relatively attractive at twenty-one and rather naïve, it wasn't something I refused immediately. His constant prodding and being urged by other waitresses kept my head spinning, but in the end, two things drove me away.

He had a reputation with multiple ladies of which I didn't want to be one, and mostly because he was married, even though she didn't seem to care about his extracurriculars. She had a beautiful home, horses, nice cars, two daughters, and everything she wanted, including a cheating husband. It didn't seem fair, and they seemed to be rewarded for their illicit behavior. When all was said and done, I just knew it was wrong.

When I was a teenager, I used to read *Star* magazine which talked about all the celebrities who were so unhappy. I vowed that when I grew up, I was going to start a company that would teach those unhappy people how to enjoy their money and put it to good use. I still feel that I could be of assistance. Time and again we hear in the news or see on the magazine racks one celebrity or another getting divorced for irreconcilability or other such nonsense, preceding the long, drawn-out battle over their finances. The media gives credence to adultery and multiple marriages and partners, which only intensifies their wrongdoing. And in the end, the money flies, and there is no joy in what they achieve because it is not God's way, but they don't see it.

Observing people around us or those in the news or media can be depressing if we only see the surface. Yes, they have money, success, palatial homes, and notoriety, but looking deeper, we might find that they have nothing of real value. In most cases God has been replaced by all that glitters, and family has been disrupted or disbanded because of all that "stuff." Someone once said that if you can't be happy with yourself, you can't be happy with others. That starts with your family members. Is it any wonder that today's world is so messed up with what *family* really means?

We all like to dream of what it would be like to have all that we could imagine, and some believe it is what they deserve. However, if God really gave us what we deserved, it wouldn't be much. Think about it. What have we really done to deserve all that God has done for us? We should be working to show our gratitude by taking care of others. "Love one another, as I have loved you." That is an impossible goal to reach, for we are human, but we still must try and stop worrying about what the other guy has or does.

CHAPTER 14

Unending Conclusion

Cancer is a venomous scavenger. Unlike other predators, it is relentless, unpredictable, and undiscriminating. It dissolves your physical, mental, and spiritual well-being. Along with taking your body on a violent voyage of drugs and intravenous feedings, disguising itself as a minimal risk, it invades the stability of the mind. From thoughts of *punishment from God* to *Why me?* to *This can't be happening*, cancer molds the mind, evading the necessary attitude to warrant healing.

They say that attitude is 50 percent of the battle against cancer. I found that to be true the first time around but not consciously. People talked about what a great attitude I had to other people who knew me and how that would get me through anything. These messages got back to me second hand. It didn't dawn on me at the time because I was so focused on survival. Of course, my faith in God assured me that everything would work out, although my human side asked, "When?'

Cancer works on your mental abilities, creating fear, anxiety, paranoia, and desperation. Someone once told me that to be holy is to be *wholly*—that is, whole of mind, body, and spirit. This second time around, my body seems to be doing well *for my age*. Truthfully, I people watch those adults who are my age, and I commend myself on my abilities. Recently, making up preliminary papers for the hospital, the numerous questions that were asked about staying on my feet, falling, breathing, dizziness, etc. left me feeling that I am in pretty good shape after so many nos in those categories. When the first cancer attacked, my mental capacity was severely altered due to my lack of confidence and frustration. I have always been an independent person, and years of single parenthood forced me to take matters into my own hands. Having cancer leaves you feeling useless and helpless.

All this brought me to the spiritual area that can be a saving grace. At the onset of cancer, it is easy to blame God or yourself (as a deserving sinner). We have all read numerous scriptures regarding God's wrath on the sinners. Funny how those passages seem to be the focus of attention while the ones that speak of God's undying love and mercy get put on the back burner. In the movie *Pretty Woman,* Julia Roberts tells Richard Gere that "the bad things are easier to believe," while he is trying to tell her what he admires about her. Many times, we carry around so much baggage that it tends to resist the truth. Other times we believe that we must have committed a grievous sin which makes us targeted by some type of punishment, such as illness.

I confess that both have seeped into my thoughts on more than one occasion, but lately, perhaps due to age and experience, I am fortified with the belief that my God is a God of love, and that He is more than willing to believe we are worthy of His love. As He has inspired writers of Scripture to profess, He loves us no matter what, and is benevolently willing to give us everything we need to endure any and every challenge presented to us. Believing, that is the hard part.

As humans, we are bombarded with the common sense thoughts and feelings that throw us off course—God's course that is. Our simplemindedness gives us the arrogance to believe that our plan is better. When cancer strikes, we panic and begin looking for excuses, reasons, and someone or something to blame. The sooner we understand that cancer is not a punishment from God any more than AIDS is a punishment for gay activities, the faster we will be able to accept God's gifts. We must assure ourselves that a gift is only a gift when it has been given and received and express our appreciation for all the gifts God continues to bestow upon us, even when we don't see them as gifts.

Life goes on and my bout with cancer is not quite over and may never be. I still have surgery coming up on two or three basil carcinomas, but they are not life-threatening. Of course, now that God has led me to these good people, I will be a regular visitor for full body scans at least four times a year (to encompass two years from the finding of the second melanoma). Undoubtedly, I now believe that everyone should be cautious about changing moles or skin blemishes, but especially light-complexioned people with blue eyes. Guilty on all factors!

This experience has brought me knowledge, thankfully, that should assist me in maintaining my health. It has taught me to be more diligent about my skin care. God has given us a temple that is our gift. We are the responsible parties for our own well-being. There are plenty of people out there that God has bestowed in our lives with knowledge and wisdom to help us with this care. We need only to take advantage of the gifts that God has provided, and not forget to say, "Thank you."

CHAPTER 15

Out of Left Field

God never promised us smooth sailing. In fact, He warned His disciples of quite the opposite. Stress, conflicts, and challenges come with life. There are no guarantees endorsed with the plans for our future. God's only offer concerning the events to come is that no matter what happens, He will stand by us.

Is that an easy concept to accept? Not on your life. We are human, and the thought of someone being available 24-7 is hard to swallow. How many people in your life have lived up to those standards? We all have busy lives, making it difficult to react instantly to those unexpected arrows that shatter the calm.

Finding that lump was a blow to the decision I had accepted to keep our lives stable, but it took a mixture of emotions when Dr. Dain stood at the end of the hospital bed, as I came out of my drunken stupor from surgery, telling me I had a fifty-fifty chance of surviving the cancer. After going through the treatment, he admitted that his true belief was more like thirty-seventy that I would even make it through the treatment. Beyond the gracious help of the Hollingers, my landlords, and people in my church, comfort came knowing I had a true friend in Jesus.

Michael's reappearance was definitely shocking, starting with a four-hour phone conversation due to our mutual friend sharing information about me. He took me back to high school days, tripping down memory lane: our first meeting, drives around town, horseback riding, time with our families, and marriages gone sour. Our first meeting was magic. No time had elapsed, or so it felt, and the gentleness of that first kiss was repeated with the latter reunion. A whirlwind of meetings and then the final quick pitch of a proposal sent me reeling. As they say, "All good things must come to an end," and they did.

After almost a year of having Michael in my life, helping him move, supporting him in job changes, planning our future and especially involving our children (we each had two), we started drifting apart. In an effort, to revive our closeness, while working out of town in Visalia, I stopped at Kmart to get some supplies and decided to call Michael, hoping to meet for coffee and a little refreshment. Stumbling over his words, he finally said, "You're making this more difficult than it needs to be."

Asking what he meant while trying to justify my actions with his complaints of us never getting a chance to get together, he threw the final strike saying, "There's someone else."

My anger took over, and I told him it was low, telling me over the phone (wall phone at Kmart) that our engagement was off. There was not much to do but drive home in tears, angry at myself for being so gullible. He called my house (we did not have cell phones back then) and my roommate answered, but after telling her what had happened, she understood why I didn't want to talk with him. When I finally did after three calls, he said he was worried about my driving while upset, and I responded that my car was all I had, and he was not worth wrecking it. Not nice, but truthful. Ironic that the next unexpected happening was my car being repossessed.

When I think back, this was definitely a message from God telling me to regroup and start over. With no job or fiancé, this double whammy sent me into deep depression, but Agnes was there for me and accepted work around the house in exchange for rent (painting, simple landscaping, and small carpentry tasks).

God does work in mysterious ways. I had been in Fresno for about two years, the amount of time the doctors had figured it took me to contract Hodgkin's. This cancer is related to environment, and they believe it to have to do with agricultural areas. Later I believed it to be God's push to get me to a place where the air was clean, the soil and water nonpolluted, and so much beauty all around that solidifies the belief that God had a hand in its creation. That was where Hawaii fit in.

Despite the struggles and job changes, my settling down at Watumull's was a God-sent. They were a great employer and gave me the support I needed, not just financially but emotionally, by having enough faith in me to promote me from receptionist to personnel to operations manager over the years. Just about the time when I was beginning to see daylight, the company decided to quit their retail division. Looking at the possibility of unemployment, I began working toward my dream of opening a horsemen's shop, complete with tack and attire. The partner I paired with was all ready to go, up to the point of signatures when his wife put a stop to the deal, and he backed out.

Once again unemployed, I was clamoring for a way to survive, not only for myself but for my son and daughter along with her daughter who had joined us. I managed to secure a job at a pool supply company as well as one at a restaurant. The pool place became near impossible when the secondhand car I had developed electrical problems and walking in from the nearest bus stop was lengthy and treacherous due to no sidewalks and minimal space along the road. Dropping that job put me on the hunt once again which led me to a buyer assistant position at K-Bay. It was an interesting job, and the people I worked with were good coworkers. Leaving the restaurant job, I took a second one at J.C. Penney. I worked in customer service and at Christmastime especially had a chance to show my creative talents in gift wrapping. Getting settled in that routine ended abruptly when corporate decided to close most of their stores in Hawaii.

Out of the blue, I found out about college classes being offered to civilians on base. I had thought, as most people, that the colleges on base were for the military and their families. Having gone to work full time at nineteen after my first semester of college, it had never crossed my mind to go back to school. Because my job at the base had basically come to a standstill and I needed a better income, I delved into the possibility of getting a degree. At the time, the state was begging for teachers. Having been a trainer of employees for years and loving the art of writing, I decided on a teaching career. Working a full-time job as well, it became plausible to utilize the excess of my financial aid to survive. Later, that would come back to bite me, but for the time being, it was a necessary evil.

Once I received my BA, I opted for a teaching position at Waimanalo Intermediate and Elementary. Just short of ten years at K-Bay, I looked forward to a new adventure. Numerous times during my schooling, I called on the Holy Spirit for wisdom and Jesus for His kind of strength and courage to carry on. Graduating Magna Cum Laude, I was blown away by the amount of blessing God had bestowed upon me.

My year at Waimanalo Intermediate was fulfilling. The students were amazing and anxious to please. They taught me lessons in survival. Their life stories were tragic by normal standards but matter-of-fact by theirs. They touched my heart and because of their strive to improve, won numerous awards for most improved throughout the year. With this type of success, it came as a complete shock when at the last staff meeting, it was announced that I was one of the teachers not returning. Later it was explained that a DOE member with tenure was bumping me. I was back to being unemployed. At least I had the opportunity to collect unemployment for a time. By the following semester, the teacher who had bumped me quit, and the school asked me to return. After that semester, at school's end, I was again bumped. It seemed at times that I was not meant to be a teacher, but just about when I was ready to give up, another opportunity dropped in my lap.

After two more schools, one as a long-term high school sub and the other teaching fifth grade, I was beginning to think that my extent of teaching was limited to a couple of years. After two years with fifth graders, on the second to the last day of summer school, the principal decided not to renew my contract. That is the deficit of teaching. Besides not being paid that well, you are only assured a year at a time. She had apparently not discussed it with hardly anyone because everyone was shocked.

As a teacher I felt invalidated, as a woman I experienced rejection, and as a Catholic, my feelings were of betrayal. This was a fellow Catholic who was denying my livelihood, and her callous approach created more irritation. To wait until the end of summer school added insult to injury, surmounting the hurt with feeble excuses of not liking the atmosphere in my classroom when she had never experienced any time within my classes. To add to the injury, she had even interrupted my time between classes during the summer asking what kind of blinds I wanted and where I wanted my SMART Board, insinuating that I would be returning. It was more than I could bear, and God heard my fury and heartbreak, but that is the great thing about our heavenly Father. He knows ahead of time what we are going to face and how we will react, and He is there to comfort us.

Finding a part-time job at a church gave me the chance for additional support since my brother was the pastor. It was comfortable; the ladies in the office were wonderful and cheered me on as I searched, yet again, for another full-time job. Since most employment is conducted online, working in an office made it easy to apply and be rejected. Because I have Yahoo, I receive a lot of spam, so deleting emails is done in a brainless fashion. Having thought negatively about one of those that kept showing up, I almost ruined my future by thinking *Christian Academy* was *Christian singles*. The Holy Spirit at work, before touching the delete button, I noticed the name *Joni* in the underline and answered the call. A very quickly scheduled interview, along with a second, and I was inducted into the orientation for new teachers. Having never taught at other than a Catholic school, I was a bit uneasy about being involved in another denomination. While deliberating, a priest walked through the office, and I told him my dilemma. He responded, "So, go there and straighten them out."

I chuckled but knew what he was referring to. There are a lot of misconceptions about Catholics.

So I went, following God's plan and hope that I have *straightened* out some attitudes or ideas about the Catholic faith. I'm not there to convert anyone, but I make no apologies for being Catholic, and for the past six years, I have answered questions honestly while working to be the best Christian I was created to be. We are all Christians and God's children, no matter how we worship.

As unexpected as this position was, I have enjoyed my class, with wonderful, pleasant students and cooperative, intelligent young people who work hard to live their faith. Going into my ninth school year, I have come to realize that sometimes the most unexpected gifts from God come out of left field.

CHAPTER 16

Just When You Think…

The follow-up to my surgeries brought about the discussion for future cancer scans. Much to my relief, I was informed that it could be done by the surgeon, also a dermatologist. Because of the melanoma, she required a scan every three months, which was the next month. The appointment came and I was prepared for the scan this time, until the nurse came in and explained that this doctor expects *everything* off, due to her check of breast and buttock areas, as well as lymph nodes, and surprisingly, feet. Although I was ill at ease primarily, the procedure was more comfortable than expected. For many women, having a female doctor is more favorable, especially for exams such as the aforementioned. For me, due to gaining weight over the past year, it is embarrassing to me for anyone to see my body, let alone another woman.

This scan found three questionable spots, which required biopsies. The lymph node check went well and the biopsies quick and easy. Going home, my thoughts wandered as I perused the idea of the two appointments made, one for three and another for six months for scans, being a bit more often than expected. Stopping by Walmart was necessary to check on a new tower for my computer, with the thought that my ten-year-old computer would not make it through this book. I handwrite my stories, books, etc. because I believe the Holy Spirit guides me better when I can connect through sight, touch, and mind. It seems ridiculous to young people, but it is how I learned to write. I began writing stories and journals at an early age, but we didn't even have a typewriter, so paper and pen were a necessity. It still pleases me to write that way.

Normally, when I've had biopsies or surgeries, calls were made from dermatology concerning my condition. But this time nothing came, and I began to have an uncomfortable feeling. Thursday, when the phone rang, I was relieved until I heard my surgeon's voice. She asked me if it was a good time to discuss the results, and I said, "Sure."

Her next statement went on to explain that two were basils, needing surgery. The third was melanoma. That word becomes frightening when you hear it. Softening the blow, she said it was superficial and would not require the lymph procedure like the first one. That was a relief. Her nurse called and set up the two appointments. I wanted it completed before school started. I have tried, ever since this thing began, to avoid worrying my students, so I have played down any doctor's appointments or bandages. Having been in tears before the nurse called but after getting the dates set up, I relinquished my fears knowing my health was in the right hands because God had led me.

Next up, surgery on two of the basils and then the big one. Arriving and dressing down to a gown, the nurse spelled out the procedure, took pictures, and left to retrieve the surgeon. When Dr. F entered, she started with an apology, saying that her nurse misinformed me. Explaining that the normal procedure was to take a half centimeter around the area, she professed that it only gave a 60 percent chance of no return, so chasing a higher percentage a whole centimeter satisfied her desired results. Since math is not my forte, that really did not provide a worthwhile visual, but my trust had grown so much for this special angel that she would have gotten my approval on just about anything.

Lying on my stomach has never worked for me and having a rubberized face wedge made it even more impossible to get comfortable. Other than that, the procedure went well until the cauterization began, and my body was jerking as the nerves were being irritated. Having always been blessed with a high tolerance for pain, it was embarrassing to bother the doctor with my discomfort. Only a few moments went by, with every effort taken to dull the twinges, and the procedure was over, once again snatched from the jaws of cancer.

So this is my life here forward. Every three months I will be subjected to a full body scan and face whatever prevails. After the three that were found, only a single basil was found on my temple. Perhaps that offers hope that the next time nothing will be found. Even if more cancer is discovered, I know that I am in very capable hands—that of a skilled surgeon and her staff, and of God Himself who has frequented my seventy years.

Speaking of seventy, my mind wanders into the *what-ifs* of the future. My mom lived to be ninety-two, while my great-grandfather exceeded her by ten years. My skin cancer, now under control, should not influence my longevity, but the newest fly in the ointment is the discovery that I have sleep apnea, which I had always thought of as just losing sleep. Going through the process, my hero cardiologist pushed me to be tested because it can cause heart problems, high blood pressure, and other ailments—things he had left out when initially *asking* me to take a little quiz for him. He is always looking out for me, which makes me feel like I am worth something. I know, from talking to other medical people, that he works that way for all his patients. God has blessed me by guiding me to the best hands in the game.

Upon taking the home test, which is relatively noninvasive, shock filled me with the results that measured 29.9 times that I stopped breathing per hour. The good news was that there was minimal loss of oxygen to the brain but left untreated could challenge that factor. Next step was the CPAP—the mask worn during sleep. The thought crossed my mind that if I ever hoped to have another relationship, it just got dashed. After reading the medical paper of causes and treatment, that last thought diminished. My old physiology teacher once said anyone who studies the wonders of the human body cannot possibly not know that there is a magnificent Creator. The more I go through these things, the more I am amazed how true it is.

CHAPTER 17

Never Alone

God created this world to be in pairs, so why is my life so designed to be single? Cursed by men who seemed to slip through my fingers, I wonder at my age whether my solitary life will continue. As I look back, the three major relationships that went awry are a touch with reality, as each of those men have since passed away. Perhaps God was trying to save me the pain of being a widow. At any rate, my future only seems to be destined for lots of time with God and no one else. Not that, that is a bad thing, but unfortunately, we were instilled with the necessity to be with others and most of the time with one special other.

Recently, when I was diagnosed with sleep apnea, it did not faze me until, on my second visit, I was shown the masks that were used for treatment. If I had ever held the hope of having someone in my life, on top of my history, why would anyone want me? With the reaction I received from Michael about my initial cancer, concern comes when considering my present dilemma with skin cancer. Most people cringe at the word and dealing with someone affected by it can be rough. I understand how they feel, but I wonder how many really consider the fear and loneliness we experience.

Having support, whether from medical personnel, family, or friends, is an especially important part of life. As we get older, the realization of being alone and the fear that goes with it is inevitable.

Finding that which makes us feel worthwhile and necessary is not always easy or feasible. Although years at business gave me great satisfaction, positions evolved into dead ends. Becoming a teacher opened avenues to create, teach, and inspire young scholars. Wanting to develop a love of writing in students was my motivation for becoming a teacher. After many years in the corporate world that utilized a great deal of my talents—creating, organization, people skills, structure, and business sense—in teaching, some of those skills have been brought to fruition; however, fulfilling God's purpose seems to be falling short.

Recently, I tried to explain how little things mount up that leave suggestions of insufficiencies. The response was that it was my own way of thinking that was the problem. I admit that I am my own worst critic, but when people say things that are hurtful (even without meaning to), undermine another's abilities, and step on toes, emotions take their toll and create feelings of uselessness. Regardless of how big or small the instances are, they suggest to us how we are not using God's gifts to His greater glory. In frustration, I remind my students that *just enough* is not good enough, and I hold myself to those same standards.

Groups of lay ministers came to our school to talk to our students, and one lady came to me afterward wanting to express her thoughts. She asked me if I was missing out in any area, which of course brought up the idea of my being single and alone. But then she, like so many others, told me I should write about my journey. I admitted to her, although I had not to anyone else, that I had started my book, and here we are. Writing, for me, has always come easy, and I attribute it to God's gift. God gave me an incredibly interesting grandfather who was also a professional artist, which stimulated another of God's gifts, taking in everything my grandpa had to share. So I grew up loving to draw and paint, but I have lost a lot of those skills due to lack of use. Teaching high school does not make way for much creativity like the lower grades, and when I have offered my help, it has been rejected (nicely, but…). My business sense and marketing skills go unnoticed, and my organizational and logistical abilities are frequently pushed aside for the *way-it-has-always-been-done* attitude.

I have been brought through my life with my faith, hard work, persistence, and the willingness to change due to a variety of adversities. I believe that God gives us the gifts we need to get through life, and that the way we use them is our gift to God. When we can achieve this, we will never be alone. There is an inner turmoil that goes on when God's gifts can stagnate. I believe the Holy Spirit keeps us on our toes by nudging us so lovingly while raising our appetite to please our Creator. This, in turn, creates that feeling of inadequacy. Our lives are supposed to be purposeful and not just in prayer. Furniture comes with *assembly required*; people come with an unseen label of *action required*. We are expected to make use of our talents and abilities, to make a difference in the world. God does not need our help to make the world a better place; He expects it.

This work to make a difference can sometimes take the place of having someone in your life. When this fulfillment of responsibility is reduced, that feeling of being alone can creep in. As Matthew tells us in his gospels, He uses the word *Emmanuel*, meaning "God is with us," in the very first gospel and accentuates its message upon the Ascension, when Jesus assures His disciples, "I am with you, always." What better covenant could we require than this direct promise from God Himself, that we are never alone.

CHAPTER 18

So Now What?

Just when situations were beginning to settle down and I became totally acceptant and comfortable with God's plan, the world became shaken with COVID-19. So many times I had watched movies that juggled pandemics as an enemy's weapon against society, but despite certain conspiracies, there does not seem to be concrete evidence of who or from where this coronavirus originated. Once, a friend told me that God does not send punishment but sometimes steps aside to allow things to happen. That makes sense actually and listening to the scientific reasoning does as well. These viruses, mostly based in the corona strain, are formed due to the methods and lifestyles of humans. Look around. God gave to Adam and Eve the responsibility of care over the earth. Seeing the loss of resources, pollution of waters, and poisoning of the air, we've done a lousy job.

Fear is a spiteful warrior, used by terrorists and other such bullies. It is what undermines the soul. Many seniors my age have been hiding out from this vicious assailant. I have reflected on so many scripture passages that command us to fear nothing but the Lord. I refuse to be fearful, but I do believe God gave us the common sense to be cautious. Mother Marianne never let fear retard her nurturing efforts to serve the lepers of Molokai, but she realized that if she and her fellow nuns became infected with leprosy, they would be of little assistance to those who were in need. This necessitated careful actions and precautions that would maintain proper hygiene. We should follow this example. There is place for caution but no place for fear. Fear is evil personified. It is the devil's greatest weapon. We should not let it control us.

Through all my ill health situations, I have come to learn and believe that God has created in each of us a well-oiled machine. Doctors and scientists discover daily new wonders about the human body and its ability to continue even when we neglect it. Our immune system is inspiring as it fights off germs, viruses, and other ailments. I have found through this treatment of sleep apnea the reality of the importance of sleep in the healing process during ailments. It is vital that we understand how during the sleep process, our body has the ability and responsibility to replace damaged cells, overcome viral infections, restore oxygen to the blood, and give the overall body the rest it desperately needs. This measure is used in extreme cases in the hospitals, as patients are reduced to an induced coma, knowing that the body heals at a greater rate in this state. When our bodies do not have to deal with the everyday challenges, they maintain a healing mode, just the way God designed.

This COVID-19 is a test of our faith. How much do we believe that God cares for us? Scripture states that He cares for the most insignificant of creatures and emphasizes that He concerns Himself so much more with us. He needs us to believe that and let go of fear. Recently at Mass, the homily was regarding fear, and Father E said that the phrase "Do not be afraid" was noted 365 times throughout the Bible. Is that pure coincidence that God has provided us with so important a message for every day of the year? That old saying arises, "There is no such thing as coincidence, just God being inconspicuous." It has been said that those things that are repeated in the Bible are important. If God repeated "Do not be afraid" 365 times, shouldn't we pay attention?

God does not make mistakes. If we had listened to Him and followed His directions, we would be living in a perfect world. However, our world is far from perfect because we are in it, and so often we think we know best. We make choices based on others, experiences, baggage we drag along but sometimes because we choose to hear what God has to say. The problem is that all those choices come with a price tag, except one. If (and I accentuate the *if*) the decisions were based on God's word, there would be no price. We just must realize that sometimes we want something so bad that we hear a voice that we think is God's but truthfully is our own. Remember, God is good. He is a God of love, and He never puts a price on His gifts. He probably would like to hear a "Thank you" now and again, but He only expects us to love one another and be the best that we can be.

Like any parent, God wants what is best for His children, and as any parent, it is nice to be appreciated. It has come to my realization that we should spend a lot more time thanking God and a lot less time being fearful of things that might be or that change our plans. Do we really have a right to constantly ask for favors? God has a plan for us, and it might include various challenges, but be assured that regardless of our fears, He is always there to lend a hand without being asked.

Through the years I've been witness to California falling into the sea, Y2K, conspiracies of JFK's assassination, 2012's destruction, swine flu, bird flu, stock market crashes, and various other supposed tragedies that were meant to befall mankind. Even those that transpired fell short of the media hype and fearful hysteria. COVID-19 is a real threat to certain people, but the spirit of fear is far more damaging than the actual virus. If we put our faith in God and take basic precautions, we will make it through this. This fear is keeping the economy from rebounding. Staying socially isolated is emotionally detrimental, especially for those who live alone and our kids. Staying away from church can begin to destroy our personal relationship with God. Many people are desperate to get back to normal, but for a time it will be a new normal. Masks are here to stay, and we will all have to figure what works, what is safe, and what makes sense. We are social beings and trying to live in isolation is anything but normal or healthy.

Trust in God, and He will deliver us. We, as in all walks of life and belief, prayed for a miracle when the COVID-19 mess started. God answered that prayer because we have been witnesses to the fastest and most efficient vaccine that was ever produced. Assuredly, the pharmaceutical companies are out to make money, but in this instance their greed was profitable health wise for the entire population. These first vaccines worked on our immune systems, which is according to God's plan. He created this body. The fact that the government stepped in to rush the process and guarantee the companies' payment was a miracle in itself. They may have been a bit more zealous than they needed to be with the country's shutdown, but they acted in good faith. They should have had more faith in God, but there weren't too many that were not down on their knees in prayer for salvation from the virus.

Since the initial actions, the nation is coming together to fight this attacker. I believe that some may be going overboard to sanitize everything there is. As any organ in the body, our immune system needs to be exercised, and all of this sanitation is not allowing it to strengthen. Too much of that and the next time something like this virus hits us, we will be totally unprotected. A little more faith in God's creating abilities and we will be on the right path. Everyone can be a part of God's plan by getting vaccinated. Some may not believe they need it, but there are those around who may be more susceptible and could use the protection. After all, that is the way we can say thank you for the gift God has provided. We can all be warriors in this fight by putting our personal feelings aside and thinking of those we hold dear or come in contact with. God wants us to help those who can't help themselves.

The greatest concern for the near future is the ideas coming from the government regarding classrooms. Someone who obviously has never been in a classroom decided that all middle and high school students should remain in the same classroom for the entire day, while the teachers move from class to class or work from home in a solitary fashion. Accordingly, they will take their breaks and lunches in the same classroom or room. This mandate also came with the order for no contact sports. As one of my former juniors stated, "I will be living in this room."

I have one crucial response to this: "Segregation has never worked."

Throughout my years, I have witnessed various times and situations where the government stepped in to regulate the relationship "problems" of society. From regulated schools and universities to bussing for improved education to telling people where they can walk, eat, sit, or even go to the bathroom, forced behavior has constantly hit brick walls. God made us independent individuals who do not like to be forced to do anything. As young toddlers, we learn the word *no* and have progressed through life using various forms of the word. Just as God did not make us His puppets, He expects us to enjoy and enforce our personal freedom. God gave us free will, so we could choose to love and obey Him, to love and serve one another, and to follow the path He prescribes for us. Even the Constitution affords us the right to life, liberty, and the pursuit of happiness. Keeping middle and high school students in the same room day after day is a disaster waiting to happen. We are human beings, not cattle to be herded into rooms and force fed.

Those in authority sometimes forget that kids are young people who are developing. They are in the process of becoming productive adults, or so we hope. This requires the necessity for them to develop interactive social skills, problem solving, and dealing with challenging situations. Creating an atmosphere of forced imprisonment does not fortify these capabilities; in fact, it negates them. This is not something in which to look forward. Not only is there great stress put on the students but the teachers as well. Just as a mother with a child in her womb passes feelings and emotions on, so will the teachers, though unwillingly, reflect their situation onto their students. Survival for all will require great faith that the Holy Spirit will guide us through this disastrous plan. Again, we must focus on success and not on fear. It will not be an easy road, but we have the promise that God will be there to give us strength and all the tools we need to win this battle.

As for me, this is a battle for which I have reservations. But with God's help, as always, I will manage to create productive lessons that stimulate learning and growth. While focusing on the academic side, I will depend heavily on God's assistance to get me through my next phase of skin cancer. My recent dermatologist visit exposed the need for three biopsies. The physician was adamant about one large growth being cancer; he just could not say what kind. As I sit here trying to complete this chapter, my mind is being scattered with texts about how the people at school are rearranging my classroom, which is a bit irritating. The call from dermatology was expected but not so soon. The three biopsies came back positive with two basils and one squamous carcinoma, which grows excessively fast. So surgery is scheduled in the next month. Contemplating the news and additional information found on the internet brought about tears, but tears are okay. Tears tend to clear the soul. When tears come, God wipes them away with His unbounded love.

These are the times when the evils of loneliness can take over. Faith in God's presence needs to ramp up, or the human frailties of depression and anxiety begin to eat away at the soul. A nurse at school has been my confidant since the beginning, so a quick email to update her quells the anguish. It is not perfect human interaction, but it helps. Taking advantage of God's angels is a must.

I look forward to getting back on track with the great surgeon who has seen me through so much. I feel comfortable and safe in her hands and His. As for *what now*, only God knows for sure, but I know without a doubt that He is always at my side and will get me through the highs and lows. He is the best friend anyone could have. Hold on to your dreams and let God make the plans.

CHAPTER 19

Okay to Dream

I'm sure that God has a creative mind and that He instilled the ability in each of us since we were created in His image. That being so, there's no reason why we shouldn't dream. If He invested a creative ability in us, we should put it to good use, shouldn't we?

Children know how to dream, many times wishing for things that make no sense or are impossible. A movie I saw was about a little girl who had so much faith in a special horse that she dreamed up what most people see as impossible. Her realistic father saw the many hurdles that the child's dream would require overcoming, but the mother saw the joy in the dream itself. Her words to her husband were something like, "So what if she doesn't make it? Let her enjoy the dream."

Unfortunately, as we get older, we seem to lose that simplicity. What harm is there in having dreams, even if they seem out of reach? If we truly believe that God provides what we need, chances are He'll come up with something that's even better.

Dreams aren't always for elaborate possessions or fantastic trips to exotic places. While fighting off cancer, watching my children endure the circumstances, I held on to the dream of being cancer-free, able to care for them as they grew. God blessed me with much more since I'm enjoying the blossoming of my great-grandchildren. Those were the dreams that kept me going.

Since our creation includes a creative side, it only figures that we are expected to use all the specialties that were implanted in us. Following your dreams carries a risk. The biggest threat comes from the fear of failure, but if you never take a chance, how will you ever gain anything beyond the present and achieve the wonders that God has planned?

Some of my dreams have gone to dust, others have come to fruition, but each situation evoked various talents or abilities that I had allowed to stay dormant. Now in my golden years, I revel at the accomplishments of those around my age, and it makes me proclaim, "Why not me?"

God gifted me with the ability to write, and although it has been my strength in business, school, and personal communications, I feel as though I haven't lived up to what God has planned for me. Life gets in the way at times, and we trudge along in our patterned way, never wanting to venture from our comfort zone. Just think if Jesus had felt that way. Where would we be?

Writing this book has definitely forced me from my comfort zone while battling fear to actually push the send button to a publisher. I've done so much writing over the years that has been put on the shelf. Something keeps drawing me back to this writing. Just when I talk myself into ignoring my computer, the little blinking light catches my attention.

I think back on the dreams I had as a child. The main one was becoming a horsewoman someday with a ranch and breeding abilities that my family could thrive on together. I lived that dream for seven years before my husband was injured. We had a ranch, complete with a custom home, five-stall barn and tack room, two children, dogs, cats, and horses. We would ride out the back of our property and ride into the hills with our kids. It was a good life, and our horse business was taking off with our first baby on the ground from our own stud and mare. Everything pointed at a bright future until it all came tumbling down.

Even then I held on to my other dreams—to start a horse program for troubled kids. I had heard of the idea being used in LA for kids from gangs who were becoming productive members of the community. Another program, run by one of my childhood heroes Ben Johnson, was doing well in Texas, where he had retired from the movie industry. Since coming to Hawaii that dream may have faded some, but financial necessities have not come available.

Perhaps that's where this book offers hope. I am a teacher, which I love, so being able to teach young people the responsibilities of being around horses would be a dream job. That's what the mounted police told our students in Waimanalo at a job fair. They stated it was the best job on the force because it was a way to utilize horses to connect with the community, especially the kids. If I could spend the rest of my useful years being around horses and helping kids, who perhaps never learned how special they really are, to create their own dreams, I believe God would smile as an acknowledgment that it's okay to dream.

CHAPTER 20

A Final Word

The word *final* is so daunting. Although this is the final chapter in His book, it is not the end. There is no end to life in Christ, and He did not promise a life without challenges. Does it seem that there are times when God is overestimating our ability to cope? Definitely, however, we just need to remember that He knows what's best for us. Just like when we were kids and our parents threw us a difficult task, we thought they were out of line. God allows hurdles to come our way, always with the ammunition needed to overcome them.

Throughout the years that I've been walking this earth, I've experienced more situations than I care to remember that could be labeled *unfair*. At the same time, I've been blessed many times over by God's loving hands that give me comfort, allowing me to move on despite the unbalanced scale.

Challenges, or how we handle them, promote growth. God made us to learn as we go through life. The choices we make may not be the best, but the consequences should, at least, teach us something. Some decisions reap rewards, mostly those that are inspired. I have always suspected that the Holy Spirit gets very frustrated with humans. He sends hints, messages, warnings, and suggestions, and we just don't get it. What a great friend who never stops trying. Aren't we lucky to have Him in our corner?

When I peruse my memories, I feel the pain of embarrassment from being evicted, having marshals show up at my work to take my paycheck for unpaid bills, hearing that my son was home when the rental place came to repossess the furniture, or even hiding from landlords when rent was due. Working two and three jobs never seemed to be enough. My ability to provide for my children continued to falter. This always promoted a sense of shame, as my futile attempts seemed to migrate into oblivion, while people around me judged without the foggiest idea of my circumstances. This is much like the way people see the homeless.

My weaknesses erupted when I looked into my children's eyes and saw disappointment. They were the driving force that kept me on task no matter how difficult the journey, and I knew instinctively that God had given me these precious gifts to create the hope that I lacked. Often, I questioned why things weren't going right and lost my feeling of control. There were times when I felt lost, only to hear God's whisper or feel His gentle touch. This contact isn't necessarily in person. I've heard so many people say God spoke to them or showed them pictures, and good for them. But that doesn't mean that the rest of us are farther away from God. It inspired and comforted me to hear our deacon explain in his homily that God didn't speak to him but still got the message to him. I believe, as in the touch I felt, that God gives us what we need. As Thomas needed proof, personification of God is required by some. He always knows what we need, but as I've said before, a gift is only a gift when it has been given and received.

Acceptance of help has always been my biggest battle. God has given me strength and talent beyond the norm, even to the point of intimidating my husband. After his injury, his ego and pride plummeted because of my abilities to take over. I simply saw a need to finish renovations, repair the roof, tractor the field, and care for the horses; I accomplished what was required. My lack of empathy helped destroy our marriage. During that time, I wasn't listening, just reacting. Rather than hearing God's voice, it seems as though I feel things or just know. In no way do I believe that it's all my wisdom, and it instills in me the sense that God is there.

When I think back to my younger days and realize how many times I have chosen, without thinking clearly and how often God steered me out of trouble, "Thank you" doesn't even come close to the appreciation I wish I could extend to my very best friend. Regardless of how many words of appreciation I relate to my Heavenly Father, I will never be able to say enough to be equal to what He has done for me.

I've always told my kids and students that our abilities and talents are God's gifts to us, but what we do with them is our gift to God. Even in my seventies I am still trying to show my appreciation by making the best of what He's given me. Going back to college for my AA in my fifties isn't something I would suggest but continuing with my BA and MED was definitely fulfilling. This past sixteen years of teaching has, I hope, brought joy to God. Even though we all need money to live on, I feel blessed to have found a career that utilizes many of God's gifts and gives me comfort in knowing I'm hopefully making a difference.

We should be grateful that God chose not to be a puppet master by giving us free will. Although He makes the plans, the fact is that we make the choices and create an imperfect world and with it comes sadness. On the flip side, however, being imperfect as we are opens up a world of fulfillment, happy tears, dreams, and triumphs. In a movie about an alien coming to earth, he said that his world had no wars, illness, or sorrow, but they had lost something. He found the spontaneity, laughter, and come-together attitude in cases of disaster refreshing and inspiring. So once again, God had it right.

I'm sure that due to my age, some that are younger think I'm way too old for dreams and assume that I will go along quietly until I fade away—farthest thing from truth. To quote Dylan Thomas, "I will not go gentle into the night." I plan to grab every breath of life I can. The dreams I have of a horse program for troubled kids is still alive in my mind and my heart. Perhaps this book will give me the resources needed to bring it to fruition, but even if it doesn't, I'll keep striving to make it happen.

Of course, taking advantage of God's grace, I long to see my great-grandbabies grow up. I'd love to own a horse again, to feel that special connection that comes with everyday contact and interaction. It would be great to travel, at least to New York, to visit my son whom I haven't seen in several years. I have an interest in seeing how California has changed, and of course, spending time enjoying the fanciful world of Disneyland.

There is a creation gene in all of us, put there by a God who loves us, and He expects us to use it. He didn't make us in His image to go through life stuck in a rut. We are supposed to enjoy life, restore the world, conquer our challenges, and fulfill our dreams. Life is too short to waste it. Bring joy to others, take care of those who need it, and relish every blessing God extends. Love life, love each other, and by all means love God.

When you look at the many wonders of the earth, it is clear how powerful and important God is. As humans, we often find ourselves wondering why God loves those of us who seem to have reached our usefulness and have nowhere else to go. Then God throws us a lifeline. Recently, I have been back in frequent contact with a very good friend. She has been my inspiration to finish this book and hopefully get it published (God works in mysterious ways). Our duty in life is to help those who need help, and my friend definitely does. I may not be the perfect one to assist her, but I can possibly get the ball rolling. Usually, she never lets me help her (pride), but we have remained friends for over twenty years, and I believe that God is trying to teach her the same lesson He taught me—to ask for and accept assistance from others when everything humanly possible has been done. God sends help in so many ways, but we must accept that help no matter what our pride tells us. He's still working on me because I have put off using the gifts He has given me to express my beliefs to those who will listen.

For everyone, God has a plan, and we often falter or get off track from that plan, but He is always there to guide us to the correct place or to clean up the mess that we have made. What a wonderful world this would be if everyone followed His guidance. This world isn't perfect and no one's life will be smooth from start to finish. Only His love is promised. Because of our humanity, there will be times when we doubt that God is with us, but as we go through life and meet the challenges ahead of us, we can only assume that He will always be there, even when we may think we are only *safe at first*.

REFERENCES

World Catholic Press. The New American Bible. New Jersey. Catholic Book Publishing Corp. 2011.

Young, Sarah, *Jesus Calling,* Nashville, TN, Harper Collins Christian Publishing, Inc. 1946

Hampsch, Rev. John. Presenter, Conference; Healing of Memories. Los Angeles, CA. 1983

Needham, Hal, Director. *Smokey and the Bandit.* Produced by Mort Engelburg. 1 hr. 36 min. 1977. VHS

Needham, Hal, Director. *Cannonball Run.* Produced by Albert S. Ruddy. 95 min. 1981. VHS

Spielberg, Steven, Director. *Indiana Jones—Raiders of the Last Ark* Produced by Frank Marshall. 1 hr. 45 min. 1981. Theater

Gains, John, Director. *Dreamer.* Produced by Luke Tollin and Brian Robbins. 1 hr. 46. min. 2006. DVD

Marshall, Gary, Director, Produced by Arnon Milchar and Steven Reuther. 125 min. 2005. DVD

Thomas, Dylan, Author. Poem; "Do Not Go Gentle." poet.org/poet/dylan-thomas. 1947

M., Pamela, Author. Poem: "Shadows That Follow." Unpublished, 1986

Weldon, Anthony. Quote: Fool me once. Presented at a political conference. 1650

Hammerstein, Oscar, Composer/Producer. Quote: A Bell is No Bell 'Til You Ring It. 1960. Google search

Donne, John, Poem Author. "No Man Is an Island." Produced as a song by Joan Baez. 1968

ABOUT THE AUTHOR

Pamela M. is presently a Christian high school literature teacher, having previously spent many years working in corporations, using her writing skills to create manuals, contracts, business letters, and projects. Corporate times were interrupted by a disease that would shatter her normal existence physically, emotionally, and spiritually. Struggling through treatment and healing, while being a single parent of two, made a new life away from California imminent. Starting over in Hawaii, which would include obtaining her AA, BA, and MED at Chaminade University in order to teach, had its own pitfalls, but the physical secrets remained untold until others sharing their experiences, encouraging her to share hers, and the Holy Spirit inspired the writing of this book.

Writing, a large part of her life, has been intertwined with her position as mother, grandmother, and great-grandmother, and as of the past sixteen years, teacher. A love of sports, especially softball, baseball, and volleyball are second only to her love of horses. Teaching and love of horses come together to fulfill her dream to start a horse program for troubled kids—namely, those who have not come to believe their true worth. Having shared that feeling, Pamela now attributes her acceptance of self-worth to her relationship with God and the assistance of the angels He has sent her way.